Table of Contents

Dedication..*v*
An Apology Ahead of Time ....*vii*
Introduction ....*xi*

CHAPTER 1   The Message 1

CHAPTER 2   The Misconception 8

CHAPTER 3   The Manipulation.............................17

CHAPTER 4   The Motive 28

CHAPTER 5   The Money 41

CHAPTER 6   The Mirror 47

CHAPTER 7   The Marching Orders 60

CHAPTER 8   The Mandate 64

CHAPTER 9   The Master 71

CHAPTER 10   The Move 80

CHAPTER 11   The Moral Standard..........................84

CHAPTER 12   The Mistakes 92

CHAPTER 13   The Manuscript 102

                      About the Author 109

Dedication

This book was written for those of you who have heard the prosperity message, acted on the principles, but have yet to come to a place of financial freedom. If you believe that it is God's will for you to prosper, but you have genuine questions and concerns about the procedures, practices, precepts, and principles that govern the message of prosperity this book is dedicated to you.

Ephesians 1:18:

*"I pray that your hearts will be flooded with light
so that you can understand the confident hope
He has given to those He called—
His holy people who are His rich and glorious inheritance."*

An Apology Ahead of Time

I need to apologize, ahead of time, as I know that I may seem to come off like a maverick in what you're about to read. I do it for one reason and one reason only:

I don't want you to make the same mistakes I did!!!

I truly want you to be as successful as the Word of God says you can be and believe, without a doubt, that what you are about to read will change your life!

You do not need to agree with what I am about to share. However, I do ask that you have an open mind and seriously consider the information I have gathered about the prosperity message. I know from experience that what I am about to share with you will help you tremendously. In fact, I wish someone had been bold enough to write about this topic years ago. I would not have wasted so much time trying to figure this out on my own. Nevertheless, revelation is here now, in written form, for those who will receive it.

Before reading this awesome book, I Must Offer You A... WARNING!!!!!

- If you expect me to sugarcoat the realities of the prosperity message...STOP READING!

- If you do not want me to call pastors to the carpet on some of their tactics when it comes to sowing and reaping... STOP READING!

- If you are expecting to hear the same old stuff you have heard preachers say year after year regarding the secret keys to living the abundant life...STOP READING!

- One thing I can promise you is that I will not pull your leg and give you *"fluff."* I cannot stand it when preachers only give you the happy ending and not the stuff in between. Why? It is the stuff in between that can weaken your faith. It is the stuff in between that kept me broke and trying to figure out why the principles I was taught were not working for me.

My style is direct, controversial, straight forward and I don't pull punches. I intend to give you the missing components to the prosperity message, so that you can make the proper adjustments in your heart, in your mind, and in your actions. I think you will like the fact that I am direct and to the point. I am sure you and I are a lot alike... you want the whole truth and nothing but the truth. We want a clear understanding of what God promises. I think you will appreciate someone who is simply going to cut through the junk and tell you what you need to know. Sometimes in life, we need someone to be direct and tell us something we may not like to hear but NEED to hear.

I can compare this to eating a big salad. It may not taste as good as a big, juicy hamburger or a steak dinner but you know it is good for you and that it is improving your health.

The same is true of the information I am about to share with you. It may not taste as good as the messages you have heard in the past. However, I guarantee you will be 100% better once you gain a full understanding of what I am trying to say. I truly care about helping you grasp the big picture and about living your life the way God intends!

Are you ready? Hope so…because the information I am about to share with you is priceless and will help you finally receive the increase you have been waiting for! Thank you in advance for taking the time to read this awesome powerful book!

Introduction

People have asked, "Why are you writing a book on such a controversial topic? What is your real motivation for doing this? Are you angry that all of the promises of God haven't shown up in your life yet? Are you trying to blow the whistle on the ministries you have come in contact with; or are you simply trying to make a buck?" The answer to ALL of the above questions is, "NO!" I wrote this book because I want to help people avoid making the same mistakes I did. I love and respect the people in the pulpit, but my heart is always to see the people in the pews grow in the things of God.

Through the years, I have come to know some extraordinary people within the Body of Christ. I have been exposed to people with great hearts, brilliant minds, and exceptional talents, who are knowledgeable in the Word yet are still struggling financially.

I know people who are so disciplined that they pray for an hour every day. I met a lady who reads the Bible for at least three hours each day. I know people who have never missed paying their tithes in over 20 years. I know a minister who is single and has been celibate for 14 years and an usher who stands faithfully at his post every Sunday and has never been late! Still, with all these wonderful and righteous deeds, the blessings of God are not tangible in their lives. Why? One of the reasons is what people are being taught. Christians are often taught that being righteous, holy, faithful, etc means automatic entitlement to wealth and blessings. We can see from some of our own lives, this is not true. This may be partially true, but it is not the whole truth.

I can give you a cup, filled with part juice and part poison. If you consume the contents of the cup you will fall dead because what is contained in the cup is only partially good for you. I was once told by a teacher, *"There is truth, there is the whole truth, and there are always two sides to every story"*.

I believe God led me to write this book because His children are precious to Him. He loves us more than we could ever know and wants us to know the whole truth about the prosperity message. Although some of us would not dare speak it verbally, God knows many of us are heartbroken. We know He cares about our souls prospering, but wonder if He cares whether or not we prosper financially.

We have experienced His healing and delivering power in our lives; yet some of us have yet to see God take us from *not enough* or *just enough*, to *more than enough*. We have worked all the spiritual principles: given, sacrificed, run around the church, touched the altar, prayed the prayer of agreement, had hands laid on us and oil poured on us yet we are still waiting on our increase.

We have seen prosperity in the pulpit. Some have seen pastors go from rags to riches, right before our eyes. We may have thought "Oh they are pastors. God has a special call on their lives. This is why God is blessing them!" However, this would mean God is a respecter of persons when the Bible says God is no respecter of persons.

Something is missing. It is kind of like a recipe your mama used to make, which you have not mastered yet. You have followed the instructions, added all of the ingredients, but it just doesn't taste quite the same. This is because your mama adds a little *something-something* to her pot that is not included in the recipe. It is this little something that gives it the flavor you've been trying to get for years. Some of us are so close. If we only add a few more things to our faith, we would experience the promised blessings of God.

When I was a child, my family was part of a church that gave us a basic foundation in God's Word. However, the pastor began to do and teach totally unscriptural things and the church began to evolve into a cult. Although my family loved the church and Pastor, we felt he had fallen *off his rocker* and we left the ministry.

Though some of the things we learned were good some were not and I still see the effects of that mindset in some of my family members. In light of this, I developed a hatred for error, especially when it comes to the teaching of God's Word. One word from God can save our lives. This same word, when manipulated or molested, can kill us. Just ask the followers of David Koresh and Jim Jones.

I hate it when we treat God's Word like a buffet and only pick out the parts we want and leave the rest. When I was growing up, I never liked *messy* people. Many times mess starts when someone shares just their side of a story. My hatred for error and my desire to give people the whole truth of God's word is the passion that drives my writing.

Sorry, but I am a bit controversial in my writing. If you follow my work, you know most of my plays, movies, etc. are somewhat controversial. I may say some things about the ministries I have been exposed to and the pastors I have come across. Please know that I am not talking about all pastors. I mean no disrespect to the preachers and teachers of prosperity. What I write in this book does not change the wealth they have acquired or the things they may have done to get it. I am only stating my opinions from my perspective and exercising my first amendment rights. I am not trying to diminish or defame pastors in any way.

The perspective of pastors may be different because of their position and all the things that must be managed as a pastor and business owner. I wish all ministers well in all their endeavors and continued success in ministry. My heart desires to teach God's people the whole truth about the prosperity message so that we can walk in victory in this area of their lives.

CHAPTER 1

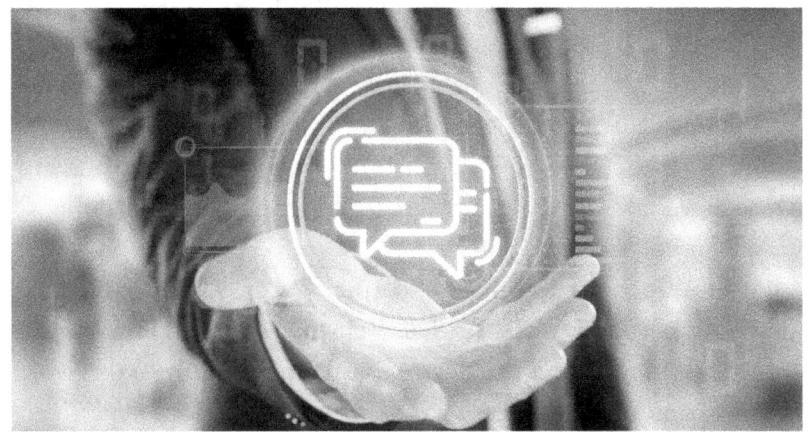

The Message

I remember when I first heard the prosperity message. It was the spring of 1999. I had recently joined a Word of Faith Church. The women at my church were planning to go to an out-of-state women's conference and I decided to go. It was my first conference and I was excited and in great expectation of learning more about God. At that time in my life, I was hungry for the Word of God. I wanted to know everything about Him. I went after God with all my heart, ready to receive everything He had for me.

I arrived on the campus of this huge ministry. I had never in my life seen a church so big! The entire campus was finely manicured, the workers were friendly, full of smiles and everyone seemed happy and excited to be there. I had never been to a megachurch or experienced such a large ministry operating with such excellence. I was even more impressed by the women who attended the conference; they were all dressed so nicely. It appeared as though they were all wealthy. Being from a city as impoverished as New Orleans, this was truly a different world for me.

I was an HR administrator at the time, making less than $20,000.00 a year. As I looked around at all of those ladies with their bling, I wondered what they did for a living to be able to afford such nice things. I began to assess my life and wondered what they knew or what they were doing that I should be doing so that I could live a better life.

I finished college, worked in corporate America and still, I was barely making ends meet. At that moment, I decided my problem must be spiritual. So, I decided to listen very carefully to the Word that was going to be taught by the speakers at the conference.

Each night there was a different speaker. As the conference progressed, the speakers got better and better. By Friday night I felt empowered with an even stronger commitment to the things of God. It was Saturday morning and I was a bit tired and ready to head back to New Orleans when there was a knock at my door. It was one of my church members asking if I was ready to go downstairs to breakfast. I was. So, I grabbed my things and was headed out the door when she said, "Don't forget your Bible." I wondered why I needed a Bible to eat pancakes. Little did I know the conference had been moved to my hotel and the final speaker would be speaking during breakfast, in the grand ballroom.

I ate my breakfast, which made me sleepy. Then, the Pastor introduced the keynote speaker, who happened to be his wife. She approached the stage, wearing a beautiful blue and white St. John designer suit, with matching shoes. Immediately, her classy style grabbed my attention. I have always admired women who carry themselves with class and dignity and this lady had both. I heard she was a prolific speaker and honestly I was expecting to hear an inspiring message, full of love and hope. To my surprise, her message was very different from anything I had ever heard. This message was not about love, hope, or improving relationships. It was about prosperity.

At first, I was a little offended. I had never heard a preacher speak so boldly in the church about money. I kept telling myself, I need to keep an open mind so I dropped my rocks and decided to chime in on what she was saying. She not only talked about money, but she also talked about wealth and the possessions she had and how God had given her all of these material things. She used Scripture and taught the Word with boldness, confidence and so much emotion.

It was as if she was a walking Bible. Scriptures just flowed out of her mouth like bullets. All of the promises about wealth and material blessing are actually in the Bible and could be received if I only believed. She not only told us about God's promises, but she also gave us principles and precepts on how to get them to work in our own lives. The crowd was electrified. Women were crying, screaming, and running around the ballroom! Everybody was ignited and ready to blast off.

I began to look around at the women in the room. I saw many of the ladies wearing designer clothes, diamond rings, and designer bags; it appeared that they had it all together. I assumed they were already doing the things she had just described in her message and this is why they were living the abundant life. After service, I immediately went to the product table and bought every book, tape, CD, and product I could find on the subject of prosperity.

I conducted an extensive study on the message of prosperity. I bought CDs and books from various preachers across the country and was very surprised at how many preachers were teaching the message of prosperity. I found an overall theme or set of rules/laws which seem to govern the prosperity message.

I. Giving.
    A. You must be a monetary giver. (Malachi 3:10)

    B. You are instructed to give monetarily to your local church. (Malachi 3:10)

    C. You must give the tithe, which is 10% of your income. (Malachi 3:10)

    D. You must give an offering. The amount is not specified. (*Malachi 3:8*)

    E. You must give cheerfully (*1 Corinthians 9:7*).

    F. You must be an obedient giver (*1 Timothy 6:18*).

II. Faith
    A. According to Galatians 3:14, all of the promises of God are received by faith; so to receive prosperity, you must learn to operate in faith (Hebrews 11:1).

    B. Faith speaks (Mark 11:23).

    C. Faith believes it receives (Mark 11:24).

    D. Faith acts on what it believes (James 2:14).

III. Prayer
    A. You must ask God to give you riches and increase (Matthew 7:7).

    B. You must believe you will receive it when you pray (Mark 11:23 & 24)

    C. You must act as if you have it until it manifests in your life.

IV. Confession

    A. You must say what the Word says concerning prosperity and confess the blessings over your life.

    B. You must never wavier in your faith. You should never speak words of doubt, fear, or uncertainty. Complaining about debt, lack, insufficiency, and not having enough is not acceptable.

    C. You must call those things that are not as though they were (Romans 4:17). You must confess your bills are paid, your debts are canceled, you always have more than enough and God always supplies all your needs.

    D. You must call wealth, riches, increase and favor to come into your life.

V. Other elements taught in the prosperity message

    A. You must give monetary offerings to the priest/pastor.

        1. *If you give to the prophet you are entitled to reap a prophet's reward.*

        2. *According to I Timothy 5:17, prophets are worthy of double honor and monetary gifts for teaching you God's word.*

        3. *You must believe in your priest/pastor, for they are a key element to your prosperity.*

    B. A seed can meet any need. *Meaning, you can sow a financial seed for any spiritual, social, material, financial, relational, family or health need in your life and God will honor it (this includes wisdom, favor, and the anointing).*

    C. The amount you give doesn't matter. Not equal gifts just equal sacrifice.

D. You can summon angelic powers to help bring prosperity to you.

E. You should give to those who already have acquired wealth and not to the poor.

F. It is okay to give openly or to announce what you are giving.

G. You should give the first-fruit seed.

H. Pay your tithes first (before bills, debt, and other expenses)

This is the message of prosperity that is often taught throughout the Body of Christ, from various prosperity preachers. Some of the elements wavier and differ from preacher to preacher but these are the basic principles they teach congregations to follow.

After the conference, my Pastor in New Orleans swiftly adopted the teachings of the message of prosperity and in little or no time, he became known as a *prosperity preacher*. The principles of prosperity were taught to the congregation repeatedly. They were drilled into us by the pastors and leadership so much that I can quote every prosperity scripture in the Bible, verbatim. I can tell you what it means in the King James, Amplified, and the Message translations!

I thought, since it was the Word of God, the message was safe and harmless. God wouldn't put any promise in His Word that isn't true or is impossible for me to have. So, I planted the scriptures deep in my heart and tried to follow each principle to the letter.

With all my heart, I thought I had found the key to success. I thought the American dream was within my reach. Going to school and getting a good education so that I could get a good job, didn't work. The success I dreamed of, to my surprise, can be found in

Christ. I knew that salvation and deliverance are found in Christ, but then I found out I could have some money too!!

Wow! My mind was blown! Without delay, I pursued what I thought was God and godly…with all my heart, with all my mind, and with all my money!

CHAPTER 2

The Misconception

God has put many scriptures in the Bible on prosperity, abundance, and the overall health and welfare of believers. It is safe to say, Christians believe God cannot lie and that the Word of God is true. However, oftentimes we have given the same credibility of the message to the messenger. In fact, we have been trained to love and honor our pastors. We believe that he or she has a special relationship with God and spends more time with God; therefore, these servants have special wisdom and insight from God that the average person doesn't have, so we simply accept everything ministers say as truth.

> **REASON 1**
>
> **Wealth stays in the pulpit and seldom reaches the pews because... we accept everything the pastor says as truth and do not study God's word for ourselves.**

It is amazing how intelligent, educated people, such as doctors, lawyers, teachers, judges, and entrepreneurs seem to turn off their brains when they enter the church house. They readily accept the words, ideas, and theories of their pastors, even when it doesn't make sense in the natural or goes against the very nature of God. It bewilders me how I turned off *my* mind and opened my heart to these things, without even blinking an eye. I know in my own experience, I truly had a heart for God and I wanted to fulfill His will in my life. In my search to know Him more intimately, I stumbled upon His promise of wealth and prosperity and I got caught up in a web of deception.

Like most Christians, we come into the Body of Christ with needs. Often the needs are financial. Just as in the natural, a baby feeds on what his parents give him; so it is true in the Body of Christ. Babes in Christ feed on the words and messages given to them by their pastor. In the church, pastors provide us with the spiritual nourishment we need to handle life situations and circumstances. He/she is supposed to search the heart of God for wisdom, insight, and words in season for his or her congregation. But oftentimes, pastors are caught up in their own needs, hopes, and desires. They come up with messages with ill motives and kingdom projects that will benefit and increase their net worth and not that of the members, who have been placed under their care.

Let's take a closer look at and break down the prosperity message, beginning with Malachi 3:10.

Malachi 3:10:
***Bring ye all the tithes into the storehouse,
that there may be meat in mine house,
and prove me now herewith, saith the LORD of hosts,
if I will not open you the windows of heaven,
and pour you out a blessing,
that there shall not be room enough
to receive it.***

Now, I was taught to believe that if I tithe, according to Malachi 3:10, God will pour me out a blessing I will not have room enough to receive. The blessing is not money falling from the sky because if this was the case, I would simply make room to receive more money. The Scripture is referring to the blessings of wisdom, insight, witty inventions, concepts, and ideas that will bring about financial increase. In this case, I can see that receiving so many business ideas could be quite overwhelming, especially if I tried to act upon every single one of them. I was led to believe that if I wanted wealth and success, I had to tithe. To the contrary, I was taught if I do *not* tithe, I was *a God-robber* and would be subject to the *curse*. The curse is not a death sentence but a financial curse, meaning, I would always live in poverty, lack, and never experience a surplus of wealth.

Galatians 3:13 says "We've been redeemed from the curse of the law." I wondered how I can be subject to something from which I have already been redeemed. Somehow all of this was not adding up. So, I began to dig a little deeper. I recall thinking about the successful people that I knew (some I knew were sinners and had not seen the inside of a church in years). This troubled me because I was struggling, trying to do what the Word of God says; while they seemed to be living it up, with no care or regard for God or his Word. I wondered how many millionaire and billionaire entrepreneurs actually gave money to their local church. I was floored when I heard Bill Gates and Warren Buffet are atheists. I wondered how can this be. They are in direct violation of God's Word. It all seemed like some kind of sick joke. I saw the wicked prospering and so many Christians struggling.

I watched the members of the church I attended (whom I knew were tithers), barely making ends meet and living from paycheck to paycheck. It is amazing how some of them paid their tithes and gave offerings during service. Yet, afterwards, asked me for gas money or to bless them by taking them to lunch. I would be like, "Didn't I just see you walk up and give the pastor a hundred dollars?" They replied, "Yeah. I am believing God for a breakthrough." What they thought was a move of faith, was actually foolish! If God really moved upon their hearts and told them to sow the money they were supposed to use for living expenses over the next few days, then they should have been confident, knowing that God would supply their needs, instead of walking around the lobby in fear, begging for someone to bless them!

REASON 2

Wealth stays in the pulpit and seldom reaches the pews because... we practice emotional giving rather than being led by the Holy Spirit.

Some preachers are gifted in stirring people's emotions and some believers sow because of the excitement of the moment and not because we are prompted by the Holy Spirit.

Have you ever been in service and the Word of God bares witness with your spirit and you felt the need to act upon the Word by giving monetarily? This exchange was between you and God and only you knew what you heard God say about your situation. You acted on what you believed.

I have been in many church services where I have seen people walk up to the altar with money and I wondered whether or not they were led by the Spirit of God or another spirit. Sometimes, the preachers will say things in such a way that you might think God is leading; however, it may be another spirit that is leading you. Perhaps there is a spirit of greed, either in you or in the pastor. It may be a spirit of desperation and you are just giving to get something in return.

Maybe there is a spirit of acceptance. Oftentimes people walk up to the altar with money in their hands to communicate to the pastor that he's preaching well. It may be a self-righteous spirit and they want to prove to everyone that they can *hear from God*. Perhaps there is a spirit of vanity and they just want to be seen and sometimes people haven't heard anything from God. They are just followers and doing what everyone else is doing.

The Misconception

Whatever the case may be when the money and the moment are gone, they are walking around the church looking crazy because they really don't know how they are going to survive until the next payday! The sad part is that this is happening to believers in churches all over the country. Week in and week out, people make emotional, irrational decisions and then expect God to fix their circumstances. Statistics show that 65% percent of Christians are in debt, have bad credit, and are living above their means.

There is such a thing called *false prosperity*. This is when Christians buy jewelry, houses, cars, and designer clothes and pretend that they have it all together when in fact, they are drowning in debt and are one paycheck away from poverty.

I have seen relationships destroyed and marriages torn apart, due to a misunderstanding of the prosperity message. One spouse feels an obligation to tithe, while the other feels an obligation to pay the bills. They dispute their differences month after month until they eventually end up in divorce court. I have also seen couples buy houses they knew they could not afford. Out of embarrassment, they left their church because their home went into foreclosure.

We have all heard the cliché *"fake it till you make it,"* but this does not mean lose all common sense. I once was in a high-end department store with a church member who purchased six dresses totaling $18,000. She maxed out three credit cards just to make the purchase. She walked into church the next Sunday with one of her new outfits on and everyone complimented her. The truth is, she had to pay dearly for those compliments and she's probably still paying for them today!

Now when I look back on everything, I see how dangerous the message of prosperity can be in the hands of preachers with wrong motives and members who don't really understand God's purpose for prosperity. I see how I was manipulated into thinking God would penalize me and sentence me to poverty if I did not give money to my church. How foolish I was to think that a loving God would place more value on my giving 10% of my income than on my overall well being. To think of God as being so harsh is not an accurate assumption of Him and not a true aspect of His character.

The saints of old, such as Abraham, Solomon, David, etc indeed gave offerings unto the Lord. However, they gave out of their obedience and love for God, not out of some spiritual mandate. There are others mentioned in the Bible, such as Ruth, Esther, Joseph, and even Jabez whom we have no record of their giving yet, they were still blessed by God. So, does God bless us based upon our giving, or does He bless us because of his love, grace, and mercy?

I believe there are many reasons God blesses us. Ultimately, it is totally at His discretion. Why, then, are we taught so adamantly that God blesses us based on the giving of tithes and offerings? Why do preachers place such a demand on us to give, as if it is the only way to receive the blessings of God? It is almost like paying for a blessing, sort of like bribing God to hook us up as if our money can actually move the hand of the Creator of heaven and earth.

Many prosperity preachers may argue this point, they may say our commitment to tithing reflects our integrity and (quote) **Matthew 25:23b:** ***Well done, good and faithful servant; thou hast been faithful over a few things, I will make thee ruler over many things.***

One may interpret this to mean: When we have proven to God that He can trust us to tithe from the money we presently have, then God can bless us with more because we have been faithful with the little. I beg to differ…our tithing reports are not a reflection of our integrity. Our credit reports are! Our credit reports are a proven history of how we handle money. Some of our tithing reports are impeccable yet our credit reports are horrible! We have documented proof that we do not pay on time and are living above our means because our debt-to-income ratios are out of balance. When we make a vow to pay our creditors, we are obligated to maintain the integrity of these contracts by keeping our word. If our credit reports are *jacked up*, then we have not been faithful stewards, based on Matthew 25:23. How can we expect to be blessed with millions, when it has already been proven that we cannot handle thousands?

I have heard preachers say, "If you want to get blessed financially, you have to give financially." Then on other occasions, I have heard the <u>same</u> preachers say, "Sow a seed for your healing. Sow a seed for your breakthrough. Sow a seed for your marriage. Sow a seed for favor. Sow a seed for your joy, peace, etc." I have even heard it said at a singles conference, "Sow a seed if you want to get married." WTH!!! I don't even want to discuss how many single people ran up to the altar with money, trying to bribe God to give them a mate.

Jesus paid the ultimate price at Calvary, obtaining for us everything we need to live a victorious life here on earth. A lot of things preachers say we must pay for, have already been purchased by the blood of Jesus and have been freely given to us. It is time out for us believing we have to sow a seed for everything. Some preachers are getting over on us but is it really their fault? Perhaps it is our fault for being ignorant. I have been told many times a seed can meet any need. Where is this in the Bible? People, we have to wake up and stop feeding on this nonsense!

Paul said it best in his letter to Timothy, "
Study to show thyself approved unto God, a workman that needeth not to be ashamed, rightly dividing the word of truth.

Hosea 4:6 says,
"My people are destroyed for a lack of knowledge."

For years people have been screaming that the prosperity message is being used to manipulate people yet we have rejected their words as if they are messengers of the devil. Now it is time to open our ears and our eyes and stop being naïve about what has gone on for too long in the body of Christ!

CHAPTER 3

The Manipulation

I am not against tithing and giving offerings, I believe they are both Godly and right. The message of prosperity is ordained by God. It is the very nature of God to desire his people to live victorious and abundant lives. However, I take issue with the way the message is being delivered. This is like ordering a package over the internet and when it comes it is late, the delivery guy is rude, my package is all beat up, dirty and bruised and I don't even want it anymore. I feel this is the way some preachers have delivered the prosperity message. The principles they use are out-dated and part of the old covenant and not the new. The pastors are rude and insensitive to the Holy Spirit and the message itself has been tainted, manipulated, and molested. Frankly, I just don't want to hear it anymore!

Maybe I am wrong, but I do not believe there should be so much emphasis on giving in the church. Christians should not feel pressured or sent on a guilt trip if we do not or cannot give. I remember dreading going to church because there was always some *giving* campaign going on.

Nearly an entire hour of the church service was dedicated to rally for the campaign. This does not happen in the course of a single day. Anyone can endure the begging for one day. I am talking about at least four to six weeks of this, culminating with the BIG day of giving!

The leadership had the members, faculty, and staff fill out pledge cards, containing the amount they planned to give. Colorful brochures were given out. Videos were shown. CDs were passed out. Members were prompted to check a specific box, indicating the amount of the pledge. The pledges were never small; they started at $1000 and went up to $25,000 plus!

Like clockwork, leaders followed up with a Scripture, such as Job 22:27. Confessions were written down and congregants were expected to repeat them to promote a feeling of spirituality and moral obligation to pay what was vowed or pledged.

Preachers use one particular story from the Bible to scare members into giving. This text is found in Acts Chapter 6. It is the story of Ananias and Sapphira. This couple sells a property and vows to God that they are going to give so much of the proceeds to the Christian community. However, they conspire to give a lesser amount and died.

The implication made from the pulpit is that God takes our giving seriously. So, we should not play with God in this area. This is what I call *pimping* at its best. Some preachers should receive the *pimp of the year* award for some of the things they say from the pulpit!

In my dumb days, when I heard this message being taught in this way, I was made to feel I never wanted to miss paying my tithes. This was not out of obedience to God's Word but out of fear of the curse.

At that time in my life, I had little money and plenty of debt. My phone used to ring all day with creditors calling. I was more afraid of the wrath of God than the consequences of having bad credit. My pastor said when he was broke, he paid his tithes and himself, but everyone else had to wait.

When I considered how blessed his life was, I decided to do the same thing, believing one day I would be rich and all my debt and bad credit would go away. Many times I heard pastors say, from the pulpit, that because they decided to pay their tithes instead of their creditors, God blessed them and we should follow their example. Almost every time this statement was made, it was followed up with:

Hebrews 6:12 which says

"That ye be not slothful, but followers of them who through faith and patience inherit the promises."

As an adult with good common sense, I should have made better decisions, but the truth was I wanted to be successful and I thought I was getting accurate information. I was deceived by my own heart, needs, and desires and I take responsibility for this. However, I also know that preachers know people are going through financial challenges and take advantage of these situations to prey upon their members.

I read a quote in a book that has always stuck with me. It says, "One person's tragedy is another person's opportunity." For example, when we lose a loved one it is tragic for us. However, the tragedy means money in the bank for the funeral home. When our cars breakdown it can be traumatizing for us but it is a golden opportunity for the auto mechanic. Could it be that some preachers are nothing more than opportunists? Could it be that during a time of recession and economic turmoil some preachers use this as an opportunity to prey upon their members? The ugly truth is, "Yes." Many mega-church ministries have huge overhead budgets, payrolls, expenses and they too are under pressure from bill collectors. Instead of liquidating their assets (such as their Bentleys, Rolls Royces, private jets, vacation homes, Rolexs, diamond rings, etc.), pastors put enormous pressure on their members to give.

I have known people who stopped going to church because they experienced stress and anxiety attacks in church, due to the pressure pastors placed on them to give. How unfortunate it is for Christians to walk out of the church house with their heads hanging down, feeling they have dishonored God because they were unable to contribute to some so-called *kingdom project*.

How disgraceful it is for preachers to put so much emphasis on giving that they send congregational members through so much emotional trauma, stress, guilt, and depression that they walk away from God's house in fear, thinking God is going to punish them.

How do I know this? I know, because I was one of these members! I have eaten at family members' homes, instead of buying groceries and scrapped up money for gas because I would rather starve and walk to work than to have God mad at me for not paying my tithes.

There have been times when my check was just enough to pay my bills. I was so afraid if I paid my bills and didn't tithe, something bad would happen to me for example, getting hit by a truck or my car would explode or my apartment would burn down…all because I was a God-robber and was now subject to the curse.

I know you may think I was a little silly but when your pastor is obsessed with the prosperity message and he talks more about the curse than the blessings of tithing, it might make you a little crazy in the head too!

REASON 3

Wealth stays in the pulpit and seldom reaches the pews because... we pay tithes instead of our bills, causing our debt and interest rates to increase.

I was also afraid that if I did not give I would never be successful in life and I would always live from paycheck to paycheck. This scared me more than anything else. My whole life seemed like a struggle, as if I was barely keeping my head above water.

I could not bear the thought of living my whole life this way. I was taught that I could live the best, have the best and go first class in life and I bought it, hook, line, and sinker! I was a consistent tither and giver of offerings. Giving became a part of my lifestyle.

Like clockwork, I gave every month. I paid over and above what was required. I even gave money I should have saved or used to pay off my debts, but I didn't care. My mindset was that I wanted to get blessed.

I gave the ministry my treasure, my talent, and my time. I was actively involved in the church and I spent almost every day at the church. Before I knew it, my faithfulness led to my pastors offering me a full-time job with the ministry.

This was absolutely the worst thing that could have happened to me! When I was in the pews I could see just so much. Once I got behind the scenes, I got a bird's eye view of the corruption and this totally threw me off. I could not believe some of the things I experienced. It was devastating to me personally, emotionally, and spiritually.

When I worked full-time for the ministry, I saw instances where the pastor fired employees because they did not pay their tithes. How insensitive for a pastor to fire a man who decided to take care of his wife, his kids, and his bills, instead of paying his tithes. Where is the love and compassion of Jesus that is supposed to be in the hearts of the men of God?

Now, this person can no longer fulfill his calling in his local church. He cannot take care of his family. He is angry with the pastor, embarrassed among his co-workers (who are also his church members), so out of shame, he decides to leave the church. My question is…how does God get the glory in all of this?

I know that pastors have a rule for their employees, if you're being paid from tithes and offerings then you must give tithes and offerings. I've spoken to several lawyers who said employees who are terminated because they refused to donate to a church organization is discrimination based on religious affiliation and it is an EEOC code violation. This practice is not only unlawful naturally, but it is also spiritually unlawful. God gives us an example of how we are supposed to give:

2 Corinthians 9:7

"You must each decide in your heart how much to give. And don't give reluctantly or in response to pressure. "For God loves a person who gives cheerfully."

When ministries force their employees to pay tithes, they are causing their employees to violate God's Word because we are not supposed to give under the pressure of losing our jobs. It's funny how pastors want to run their churches like corporate America but then stick in religious rituals where it's profitable for them.

In corporate America employees are not terminated because they refuse to invest and buy stock in the company. Why is it that in the church, employees in the ministry fear the risk of losing their jobs if they do not give 10% back to the company they work for? In all fairness, churches should pay their employees 10% more than corporate America since employees must give 10% of their salary back to the church.

Here are some more examples where preachers went too far:

- I have been in services where the pastor said, "The Word will not go forth until the budget is met." He stood there silently and waited until people put money in the bucket.
- I was once in a service where the pastor actually pulled out a list of the names of the people who were not tithing. He called the names out and embarrassed the people in front of the whole church.
- I have heard of churches having *cash for gold campaigns*, selling prayer cloths, and having members put their tithes and offerings on credit cards.
- I heard a pastor say that he wanted to shoot all of the members of his church who were non-tithers because they were stopping the flow of the anointing in the services.
- I heard a preacher tell the members they needed to sell their stocks and bonds, go into their retirement, mutual funds, 401ks, and savings accounts, and bring an offering to the church because God has need of their money.

- I have seen Christians lay fur coats, diamond rings, watches, family heirlooms, televisions, and laptops at the altar because the preacher used a Bible story to manipulate them. In II Kings chapter 4, the prophet asks the widow what she has in her house that she can <u>sell</u> to get out of debt.

This preacher turned the story around and asked the church what they had in their house that they could <u>sow</u> to get out of debt! The next Sunday people brought all these personal and valuable items from home to sow in exchange for supernatural debt cancellation. The pastor simply loaded up the church van, took the items to the pawnshop, and cashed in on his member's prized possessions!

Now, let me set the record straight, I do not believe ALL preachers are predators but I do believe that some are. I do believe that some use the Bible as a pistol to rob their congregations. I believe that the scriptures God has placed in the Bible to benefit us, have been intentionally used by some preachers for their own benefit.

I know of some preachers who paid $5000 to sit in a seminar for the purpose of learning strategies on things like: influencing their members to give, the art of taking up an offering and what personal items they should and should not buy with the church's tithe money. It was basically a seminar for preachers on how to *get over* on their members legally, without being audited by the IRS.

I have visited websites of professionals whose sole purpose is to teach pastors tactics on influencing their members to give. I understand that tithes and offerings are needed to help ministries function and operate, but I do not believe that ministers should use fear, intimidation, and guilt to meet their ministry goals and budgets.

The sad part is these types of things happen every day in the Body of Christ, but no one wants to say anything about it. We have been trained to pray for and to cover for our leadership. We have incorporated codes of silence and expect God to quietly fix all of our issues.

But what about the people who have been hurt, offended, and scattered at the hands of those proclaiming to be Christians? What about the Christians who are unfruitful not because they are trapped in sin, but because some of the principles they were taught and acted upon do not line up with God's word; therefore, God can not honor it? What about the people who have lost their homes and marriages trying to acquire the material possessions that preachers tell us the righteous are supposed to have?

If I could have recorded the conversations and prayers I prayed to God that were made in my state of confusion, all of the times I went to the leaders of the church and asked them if I was doing something wrong because I wasn't seeing the abundance the pastor said I should have if I worked the principles of prosperity.

All of the nights I sat contemplating the faith while being taunted by the enemy because my bank accounts were dwindling. I was tormented in my mind because I did everything I was told to do and I still wasn't seeing the results. My desperation made me even more gullible and open to giving. The pastor used to say, "if what you have is not enough to meet your need, then it's a seed. You should give it to God and He'll multiply it."

Like many Christians, I've walked away from altars with tears in my eyes, knowing that I just gave my very last. I thought everything I was being taught was right because the pastor had a Bible in his hands.

A pastor said something in his arrogance one day. He said that people will believe anything and they will give to anything, and he was absolutely right. The whole truth is, the prosperity messengers have made Christians both gullible and passive. Gullible because we believe and give to everything they say and passive because after we've acted on what we believed, we think that it automatically attracts and brings wealth into our hands.

Even in my ignorance, God never let me go hungry or homeless. Nevertheless, I was still being led by the *spirit of greed* and not by the Spirit of God.

CHAPTER 4

The Motive

Motive is something that causes a person to act in a certain way or do a certain thing. It is the goal or object of a person's actions.

In this chapter, we are going to get down to the heart of the matter. I will not sugar coat anything or make excuses for anyone, including myself. We know the subject we have been discussing is prosperity and when most people hear the word prosperity, they automatically think money.

In fact, most of our lives are dedicated to the pursuit of obtaining money. Think about it. Why is getting an education important? It is important so that we can get a good job and make money.

Why do we work 40 to 60 hours each week? We do it so we can get a paycheck and make money.

Why do professional athletes train extensively for so many hours each day? They train so they can perform at high levels and make lots of money.

Now that we have established that obtaining money is the obsession of 99.9% of people on the planet, let's relate it back to the subject at hand.

When preachers begin their ministries, in my opinion, most really have a heart for God's people and want to please God. Oftentimes they struggle in the beginning and have awesome testimonies of faith about how God provided for them and the ministry during very difficult times.

New preachers are like new babes in Christ. They are on fire for God. They want to tell everybody about Jesus and help as many people as they can. There are so many hurting people around the world today that when they see the fire, passion, and compassion bursting from these men of God, they are naturally drawn to them.

Before they know it, the church begins to grow. Many times, when churches experience exponential growth, preachers begin to drift away from their original mission and start looking at the math.

Let's say you have a church with X amount of members. Out of all the members, you can get only about 50% of them to tithe. The average American household income in 2010 is $38,000 per person. The 10% tithe from this amount is $3,800. Let's do the math, ranging from the membership of a small church with about 200 members to a megachurch with 30,000 members.

Members	50% of Members Are Tithers	Members Annual Tithe	Church Annual Income
200	100	$ 3,800.00	$ 380,000.00
2000	1000	$ 3,800.00	$ 3,800,000.00
5000	2500	$ 3,800.00	$ 9,500,000.00
10000	5000	$ 3,800.00	$ 19,000,000.00
20000	10000	$ 3,800.00	$ 38,000,000.00
30000	15000	$ 3,800.00	$ 57,000,000.00

The chart above is based on the tithe of a congregation with an average income of $38,000. In some churches, the incomes may be greater or lesser, depending on the education and professional levels of its members. This chart does not include offerings that are also given by church members. Nevertheless, these numbers are staggering and can sway even the most honest of preachers, when they consider how much money they can make.

Large profit margins may account for the reason the prosperity message became so popular a few years ago. When pastors begin to look at the numbers, one can see how their motives can change from fulfilling the great commission to filling every seat in the church. One can also notice that instead of preaching and teaching on all of the promises of God, preachers focus on prosperity, with an even more intensified focus on tithing. Not all preachers are moved by the numbers or the math, but believe me, some are.

I remember when a certain pastor was on fire for God! He taught God's Word with simplicity and understanding. Miracles were taking place, demons were being cast out and everyone was learning and growing in the things of God. Then, he became *a son* of a noted prosperity preacher and everything changed. He got so inspired by the material wealth and blessings his spiritual father had, that he went after those things with all his heart. This was the worst possible thing he could have done in his ministerial career because his motives changed from wanting to be more like Jesus, to wanting to be more like his spiritual father.

His spiritual father had a mega-church with over 20,000 members in multiple locations. So, he could afford the Bentleys, Rolex watches extravagant homes, and to buy his wife diamond rings and designer clothes. This pastor's church membership was under 700 yet he endeavored to do the same as his mentor. He bought a Bentley, Rolex watches, an extravagant home. He bought his wife designer clothes, diamond rings and he opened a second campus at a different location.

All of these extra expenses put the ministry under a financial strain. In turn, he had to put the membership under enormous pressure to give, so that he could maintain his ministry and lifestyle. All of his messages were now about prosperity, wealth, and financial increase. And like an infectious disease, the spirit of selfishness began to spread throughout the ministry.

Since selfishness is the opposite of love, all other types of spirits began to creep into the church, such as jealously, envy, strife, divisions, backbiting, evil speaking, divorce, adultery, fornication, etc and before you knew it, the whole infrastructure of the ministry began to collapse. Eventually, Hurricane Katrina washed it all away on August 29, 2005.

> **REASON 4**
>
> **Wealth stays in the pulpit and seldom reaches the pews because... we are more loyal to our pastors than we are to God. We continue to sow into bad ground, even when we see our pastors are no longer following Christ.**

One might think surviving the most destructive storm in recent American history would have been a wake-up call for this pastor but it was not. Ironically, after the storm, he and his wife compiled a list of phone numbers of the church's rich and affluent members. They called them to ask how they were making out since Katrina and if they would continue to support the ministry financially. Some agreed and some did not.

However, it amazed me that they did not bother to call and check on anyone else except the people they felt could help maintain their lavish lifestyle. The rest of the people (who may not have had a lot of money but were faithful to the ministry) did not seem to matter. It was not important to him that they were displaced, lost their homes, jobs, and even some family members in the flood. If they were not giving hundreds of thousands of dollars to the ministry each month, they had to fend for themselves.

During this time, many pastors set up churches in other cities so they could still keep in contact with their displaced members. This pastor did the same. The problem was he never came to see his members. He had an associate minister to teach them each week. The only time he came to minister to his displaced members, amazingly, he taught a lesson on why they should tithe from their FEMA money. It was more than obvious that his motive had shifted from a love for God and God's people to a love for money.

I Timothy 6:9-10 explains it best.

"But people who long to be rich fall into temptation and are trapped by many foolish and harmful desires that plunge them into ruin and destruction. [10] For the love of money is the root of all kinds of evil. And some people, craving money, have wandered from the true faith and pierced themselves with many sorrows."

Another thing I have heard preachers talk about which really troubles me and clearly shows their ill motives is in regards to the principle of *sowing upward*. I have heard preachers say, "You must give to someone greater than you or more successful than you so that their blessings or anointing will come upon you."

This is a bunch of foolishness that has no Biblical root whatsoever! The reason preachers say this is because, once again, they are trying to get people to give them money. When you build churches in low economic areas, oftentimes the richest person the members know (who is not a drug dealer), is the pastor. This is nothing more than a ploy that puts cash directly into the pastor's hands, without anyone having to check a box or lick an envelope.

If this principle is both Biblical and true, we would be able to find it being done in the Scriptures. And Jesus' ministry would have been the richest ministry to ever grace the planet since he is the greatest and most successful preacher/teacher to ever walk the earth. Anyone smart would have given everything they had to His ministry to be a partaker of His anointing.

I'm sorry. My bad! This was done in the scriptures but the outcome was very different from what preachers teach.

Acts 8:18-22

¹⁸ When Simon saw that the Spirit was given at the laying on of the apostles' hands, he offered them money

¹⁹ and said, "Give me also this ability so that everyone on whom I lay my hands may receive the Holy Spirit."

²⁰ Peter answered: "May your money perish with you because you thought you could buy the gift of God with money!

²¹ You have no part or share in this ministry, because your heart is not right before God.

²² Repent of this wickedness and pray to the Lord in the hope that He may forgive you for having such a thought in your heart.

Okay, I admit it. I gave Bishop Big Shot and Prophetess Penelope money based on this pitiful principle. No wonder I never received my helicopter, my mansion, or my increase. Wow, do I feel like an idiot! I know I was not the only one slapping money into their hands. If this is you, don't say a word. Just look straight ahead and keep reading!

You will notice Peter says Simon wants to buy the anointing because his heart is wicked. Preachers know some of their members are just as money-hungry as they are, still they use our ignorance to make a profit. They have already read this Scripture in Acts. They know and understand the anointing and the gifts of God cannot be bought, sold, or transferred with an exchange of money.

The Motives

The gifts of God are freely given to us. We do not have to pay for them. If God wants to make you rich and successful, there is nothing you can do about it. It was freely given and freely, you receive it. How dare a preacher try to pawn it off for a few thousand dollars, from a bunch of broke naive Christians, trying to get rich quickly? How dare we try to purchase something that has already been purchased by the blood of Jesus?!

Our hundred dollar offering does not compare with what Jesus sacrificed for us at Calvary. How do we even know if we want pastor so and so's anointing? We do not even know what spirit he represents. All we know is what we see and what he has. Furthermore, we do not know what was done to get that big church and that fancy car. We, in the body of Christ, have to stop being so impressed by people and their stuff!

If it is possible to receive an anointing of success and it can be transferred with an exchange of money, I would surpass everyone in the Body of Christ and give all my money to Bill Gates. He clearly has more success than any preacher.

Yet, preachers say we are supposed to sow into *good ground* and a successful preacher's ministry is *good ground*. Once again, if this was true, I would have more anointing and success if I gave my money to the Pope and the Roman Catholic Church because they are the most prosperous ministry in the world!

The story of Elijah and Elisha is used to justify the transfer of the anointing. As I recall, Elijah does not tell Elisha he has to give him money to get the double portion. Elijah says (paraphrased) "Just watch me, do what I do. Follow me as I follow him and when he takes me and you are following us, you will receive the double portion."

Another popular prosperity message passage used to justify the exchange of money is found in Matthew.

Matthew 10:41(KJV)

He that receiveth a prophet in the name of a prophet shall receive a prophet's reward; and he that receiveth a righteous man in the name of a righteous man shall receive a righteous man's reward.

To receive a prophet is to respect the office or position he stands in and God's calling on his life. When you receive a prophet, you do so by showing him kindness and favor when he comes to your town. This Scripture has nothing to do with an exchange of money. When we see the word *reward* we automatically think money. Just because you give money to a pastor does not mean that you are gonna experience life the way that he does. We, as believers, have to stop being lovers of money ourselves. This is how we are so easily deceived.

Here are 7 Keys to determine Bad Motives in Preachers:

1. When the pastor uses questionable and unscriptural means to get the congregation to give.
2. The church never does outreach or anything to help the community.
3. The majority of the messages have something to do with financial prosperity and giving.
4. The pastor associates receiving spiritual gifts with giving monetarily.
5. There are no programs or ministries in the church that help the members to build wealth and strengthen financially.
6. Building projects never come to fruition, even after the financial budgets for the projects have been met.
7. When the pastor is more concerned about the church growing in members, than the members of the church growing spiritually.

Here are 7 Keys to determine Bad Motives in Ourselves:

1. When we give only to get something in return.
2. When we think that financial increase is only to lavish ourselves with material things.
3. When we buy houses, cars, clothes, and jewelry prematurely, just to be seen.
4. When we tithe out of fear instead of faith.
5. When we exercise spiritual principles and are not willing to do the natural things that attract wealth.
6. When we acquire wealth by questionable means and not by walking in integrity.
7. When we give tithes and offerings but are still holding on to sin and unforgiveness in our hearts.

When I think about motives, I have to consider myself, in regards to the prosperity message. Why did I do what I did? Why do I have what I have? I can very well blame the preachers for having bad motives, coming up with their own theories, lacing their pockets with the Lord's money, and manipulating the Word of God.

In all of this, God judges the heart. He knows what is really happening on the inside of the believer. I feel he will still honor my 10+ years of consistent tithing and my offerings which totaled into the tens of thousands, if my heart is right. Yes, I loved God, wanted to do His will, and even had kingdom assignments ready to be executed had I ever received a surplus of wealth.

Yet, underneath all of the righteousness, there was a wrong motive. The truth is, I was tired of living from paycheck to paycheck, tired of being broke, tired of working for pennies, and never having enough money to buy nice things for myself. I heard God could make me rich and I went for it.

I read that wealth and riches should be in my house and I wanted the wealth, the riches, and the house! There is nothing wrong with wanting a better life for ourselves. God wants us to have a good life but when we are going about it the wrong way, it never works out.

James 4:3 says

"When you ask, you do not receive,
because you ask with wrong motives,
that you may spend what you get on your pleasures."

We would like to blame the preachers and call them greedy, yet we never identify the spirit of greed operating in our *own* lives. Many Christians only give to get. Our motives are not to build the Kingdom of God. It is about building our own Kingdoms, establishing our own wealth, and bettering our own lives.

The preachers have the upper hand because all they have to do is drop the bait, which is the Word of God, wrapped up in the wrong motive, then give it to a congregation of people with wrong motives, and before they know it, there is an altar filled with money.

At least the preachers have a game plan. They know exactly what to say to fill those buckets week after week. The problem with believers is, we give our money, go sit on our buttocks and wait for somebody to knock on our doors with a million dollars. We act as if our giving report is a lottery ticket and we are just waiting for God to call our numbers and bless us!

> **REASON 5**
>
> **Wealth stays in the pulpit and seldom reaches the pews because... we operate in the spiritual principles of prosperity but do nothing in the natural to bring prosperity into our hands.**

I found this to be true of myself. I had all this faith, gave all this money, and applied no action. It was easier for me to sow a seed than to read a book. It was easier for me to make a faith confession than to write a business plan. It was more convenient for me to pray in the spirit than to put into motion the witty inventions and creative ideas God had placed in my spirit. It seemed more Godly to volunteer at the church than to do what God told me to do.

God's Word is true. The *windows of heaven blessing*s were opening over my life. I just didn't act on them. My motive was to get rich quickly and not have to work at it.

So, I just sat there being lazy, still broke, questioning God and wondering why the prosperity message wasn't working for me. The problem was not with God, His Word, or the pastor. The problem was with me.

I can say all I want that I was *hoodwinked, bamboozled* and the pastor *dropped the pigeon on me*. The truth is that I serve a God who sees everything! It does not matter what the pastor does with the money once I have given it. God alone, sees my obedience to his Word and He blesses me accordingly.

He gives the wisdom. God gives the insight. He provides favor but if we fail to act, all we did was give our money away. We can shoot the pastor the bird as he drives past us in his Bentley, if we want, but the truth is, he had a job to do and he did it. He had a plan and he executed it. He sold something and we bought it. This is called *doing business!*

Now, he may have used some persuasive words. He may have used his wit, charm, and some questionable means to make the sale, but the bottom line is…we bought it!

If we knew that our motive was right when we sowed our seed and we did it out of obedience to God's Word, then God is obligated to bless us, based on the condition of our hearts.

He has poured us out the blessing, but what are we doing with it? If the business idea God gave you is still in your heart or on your mind, then you have done nothing with it. If your feet and hands are not busy trying to bring the idea to pass, then you are sitting on your financial increase and it is not God's fault!

Matthews 11:12 says:

"and from the days of John the Baptist until now the kingdom of heaven suffereth violence and the violent take it by force.

When are we, as believers, going to take what God has already provided for us? The blame game is just an excuse. We may have valid reasons for blaming our tests, trials, tribulations, and teachings to justify our present lack and insufficiency. But God's Word is still true, valid, creditable, valuable, and worthy of executing.

We have to be dogmatic about the promises of God and go after them with all our hearts! STOP Praying! STOP Fasting! STOP giving and STOP making faith confessions, if you are not going to pursue God's promises with passion, persistence, and conviction!

God loves us and his promises are not only for the people in the pulpit. They are for all who will believe and act on them!

CHAPTER 5

The Money

One of my favorite movies is *New Jack City*. It amazes me how one man, *Nino Brown,* took over an entire housing project and made it a catalyst for his multimillion-dollar drug operation. Most people would frown upon the way Mr. Brown made his money. The truth is, money has no moral conscience or obligation. It flows into the hands of whoever is attracting it. You can be a teacher or a prostitute, a drug dealer or a priest, a lawyer or a pornographer. It doesn't matter.

If you are doing what it takes to channel money into your life, money will come to you. Being a moral, spiritual, good upstanding person alone is not enough. It may be enough in a moral, honest, good, and fair world but we don't live there. If you want to argue and fantasize that this is the way the world *should* work, fine, but don't suggest this is the way the world *actually* works. Trying to impose personal standards of good and bad, moral or immoral, righteous or unrighteous, deserving or undeserving onto money is absurd.

I know this is a hard pill to swallow, especially if you have ever heard the prosperity message that is being taught throughout the Body of Christ. When God gave me this revelation about money, I literally had to get picked up off the floor because this was altogether different from what I was taught!

One of the biggest myths in the church today is that being the *righteousness of God* automatically entitles us to wealth and prosperity. This is one of the most misleading statements that can ever be made from the pulpit.

The ugly truth is, being a good person, having morals, values and integrity does not automatically entitle us to wealth, nor does it strengthen your wealth attraction. If we think we should be financially rewarded because we are honest, hardworking, faithful to our mates, good parents and are kind to animals, then we will have very disappointing lives! If we think God is going to give us wealth just because we are saved, filled with the Holy Ghost and tithing, we will eventually become angry with God!

> **REASON 6**
>
> Wealth stays in the pulpit and seldom reaches the pews because... we think being the righteousness of God automatically entitles us to wealth and prosperity.

I remember taking a ride with a church member, whom I knew was sleeping with a married man. In her excitement, she pulled out a check she had received from one of her clients for a week's worth of work. The check was over $30,000. She was shouting and praising God, and I was speechless!

Call me a hater if you want. I was not angry with her, I was angry with God! I went into my self-righteous plea...*I NEVER missed paying my tithes, I always gave over and above my normal tithes and offering, I was actively involved in over six different ministries in the church, I was celibate, I had an active prayer life, I read and confessed the Word every day and I'm still broke!* I could not understand why God favored an adulterer over me.

I even approached the throne of God with an attitude like, "God, what's up with this? Don't you see her sleeping with this married man? She doesn't even deserve your favor and blessings."

But the common denominator to her increase was not God's favor. It was the work she had done to attract the money to her.

I was taught that if I am the righteousness of God, I am supposed to be blessed and I have an entitlement to prosperity. The word *blessed* means *empowered to prosper*. It doesn't mean you *will* prosper, it just means you are *empowered* or have the *ability* to prosper.

For example, someone can give me the keys to a brand new Rolls Royce. Without a doubt, they have empowered me to drive this awesome car. However, if I simply hold the keys in my hands and never get in the car, start it and drive off, I have done nothing with the empowerment or ability given to me and I will never experience the luxury of this new vehicle.

Being the righteousness of God and doing righteous deeds gives us merit and honor in the Kingdom of God and in the Kingdom of Heaven, but not necessarily here on Earth.

As Christians, we have failed at separating spiritual things from carnal things. Money is carnal. It is nothing more than a tool or a resource we use here on earth. The amount of money we have determines the level to which we live our lives; however, our wealth and material possessions have no Heavenly value.

God doesn't care about the amount of money we have. He is concerned about our souls. So, when God looked at me, a single person, who had just enough, but was living a holy lifestyle compared to a single person who had more than enough but was trapped in fornication and adultery, in God's eyes, I was more prosperous — though, in the natural, she had more money.

God's definition of prosperity and man's definition of prosperity are very different. When God says prosperity Scripture indicates, God thinks *total life prosperity*. When a man says prosperity, he thinks of money. If we want to receive financial prosperity we have to understand what money is and is not.

We must understand the very nature of money... how it is acquired and how it moves about from one person to another. Money does not have a conscience. It doesn't know if you are a prophet or a pornographer. It doesn't know who you are, who your daddy is, what your religion is, your race, nationality, creed, or sexual preference and it does not care!

Money doesn't have feelings, emotions, eyes, ears, legs, morals, or values. Money is neither saved or unsaved...righteous or unrighteous. If money or the movement of money functioned on these things, every evil person in the world would be broke. Money would stop, pump the brakes and say, "You are doing something that God does not approve of and I am not coming into your hands!"

Money is just paper. It only moves into the hands of those who are doing what it takes to attract it. This doesn't mean making some faith confession! Stop saying "Money cometh" because money does not have ears. It cannot hear you!

You can call it all you want, but it will not answer until you do what it takes to attract it. Just because you have been meditating on financial increase and prosperity Scriptures day and night, does not mean you are going to experience financial increase.

1 Corinthians 15:46 says:

"However, the spiritual is not first, but the natural, and afterward the spiritual."

Praying, fasting, giving, confessing, and meditating on God's Word are all spiritual disciplines that should be used in conjunction with the natural elements of working, investing, inventing, producing, creating, trading, and doing business. These are all the things that attract and bring money into your hands.

The Bible tells us *"Faith without works is dead."* We can have all the faith in the world for financial increase but until we apply action to our faith, all we have is hope. Faith is acting on what we believe. Since we are the righteousness of God and know we are blessed (empowered to prosper), start that new business, invest in real estate, provide a service, buy, trade, and sell! These are the natural things we should do based on the spiritual promise of financial increase.

As believers, we have to realize we are simply *empowered* to prosper not *entitled* to prosper. We have rights but these rights must be exercised. So never find yourself quoting the following verse…

Proverbs 13:22:

*(a good man leaveth an inheritance
to his children's children:
and the wealth of the sinner is laid up for the just)*

…if we are not doing anything to attract the money that has been laid up for us. Bill Gates and Warren Buffet may be atheists but they are not going to knock on our doors and hand over their wealth to us. We must do something to cause wealth to come to us!

CHAPTER 6

The Mirror

Many days I remember being angry at God because I thought He had forgotten about me. I could not understand why so many wicked people were prospering. More than this, I did not understand how so many Christians were doing unrighteous things and going unpunished. It seemed some were being rewarded, while still in sin.

I have seen Christians engage in all types of sins: drugs, homosexuality, orgies, adultery, lying, cheating, stealing, profanity, and pornography. I have seen pastors cheat on their wives and husbands, lie to their congregations, heap up money for themselves and their families and treat God's people like servants and slaves, instead of children of God.

I have been treated as if my time, talent, and sacrifice meant nothing to the ministries I worked for. Yet, I knew I was working with all my heart. I've heard different pastors say that they pay their employees better or equivalent to what the world pays but in my case, this was not true.

When I worked for the ministry, I was paid $4,600 less than I made on my previous job. When I asked the pastor for the industry-standard salary for my job duties, I was told that it was not in the budget. Yet, shortly thereafter a Bentley and a mansion were purchased for the pastor.

I even remember going to a pastor for advice on how to increase financially. Instead of giving me wisdom and instruction, he made a pass at me. I was so distraught I went to the restroom and threw up!

> **REASON 7**
> **Wealth stays in the pulpit and seldom reaches the pews because... we get weary in well-doing and give up before we receive our harvest.**

How is it that I was working day and night to advance the Kingdom of God and could barely afford to buy items on the dollar menu? I was angry at God because I knew that He could see all of these things yet I received no Word or instruction from Heaven.

I knew He could see the evil ways His shepherd's were treating the sheep and the deception and sin that was going on in the Body of Christ. I knew He could see how the wicked and unrighteous were rising and flourishing, and faithful Christians were constantly struggling.

Satan tricked me into believing God just didn't care. So, I decided not to care. I went from being faithful to my church, to not going to church at all. I went from being a consistent tither to not tithing at all. I went from praying every day, to going weeks without talking to God. I went from living a holy lifestyle to living in sin. I went from being a woman of faith to living in constant fear… all because of a misunderstanding of the prosperity message.

REASON 8

Wealth stays in the pulpit and seldom reaches the pews because... we do not understand money and how it works.

Proverbs 4:7:

"Wisdom is the principal thing; therefore get wisdom: and with all thy getting get understanding."

Though I knew all of the prosperity scriptures verbatim, lived by the principles, and tried to keep each one to the letter, I still did not have a clear understanding of money, business, and how it worked and operated. This is why I had such overwhelming frustration and disappointment.

I have so much talent, yet I have had so many of my business ventures fail. So many promised opportunities never came to fruition and so many business deals have gone sour. I felt God just didn't want me to prosper!

I had experienced His healing power in my life. I have been delivered from sin. I had even seen Him answer prayers for people I had prayed for. However, the deep desires hidden in my heart (that I had spoken only to Him), I never saw come to pass and I was heartbroken!

I wrote a play called *The Trial of the Century*. In this play, Jesus was on trial. He had to prove to the world that He is a hero and Savior of the world. Satan is the prosecutor and he has all types of evidence that Jesus is a fraud. In one of the scenes, Satan is badgering a woman on the witness stand, named Linda. Linda is a representation of everyone in the Body of Christ and Satan is

The Mirror

trying to prove Jesus has let her down. Here is an excerpt from the play:

Lucifer: Linda, Linda, Linda why are you sitting on this witness stand pretending to have it all together? Stop fronting like everything is alright in your life when you know that's not the truth.

Linda: What are you talking about?

Lucifer: Come on Linda! What about all of your unanswered prayers? All of the nights you spent on your knees begging, pleading, and drowning in your tears? All of the time you wasted working and serving in the ministry. All of the seeds you've sown, with no return, and all of the confessions you say repeatedly that still haven't come to pass in your life. You have faithfully done everything Jesus told you to do and you still haven't been rewarded.

Linda: That's not true.

Lucifer: Stop looking at your situation through the eyes of faith and see it for what it really is. Where is your son, Linda? You wanna know where he is...? In the crack house where he's been for the past five years. Oh and is your daughter still taking her meds for Herpes? You may have been delivered from drugs and promiscuity but your iniquities left you and were transferred to your children. What happened to the house and the car you've prayed and sown seeds for? How stupid you must feel that your pastor drives a Bentley and you have to ride the bus, cause your car keeps breaking down on you. Where is the job Jesus promised to give you? You've been laid off since January. It is April. Why aren't you working yet? And how are your finances, Miss Linda? You wanna know how they are? You're basically broke. I hope you still remember how to drop it like it's hot cause you might need to shake your moneymaker to pay your bills next month. Your honor, I submit to you Linda's bank statements. Linda **will** you please tell the jury your account balance.

Linda: Three hundred dollars!

Lucifer: Three hundred dollars! That is all you have left to your name with no job and no husband. Linda has been waiting on Jesus to give her a husband for over ten years and she's even been celibate. You would think that her faithfulness would mean something to Jesus, but it doesn't. No wonder she's turned to pornography for stimulation. Oh, I'm sorry, you probably didn't want Jesus to know about your little issue. He already knows Linda but he doesn't care! He has never cared about you!

Linda: He does care! He's brought me through many tough situations.

Lucifer: I'm not talking about him paying your car note or healing you from a headache. I'm talking about the stuff that really matters to you like your crack head son, your hot-to-trot daughter, and your brother, who's rotting in jail for a crime he didn't commit. (Linda starts to cry & Jesus stands) Don't cry! Ask him! Say, "Jesus what about me? What about the prayers I prayed? What about the promises you made? When are you gonna remember me and bless me like you said you would?" Ask him if you even matter to him at all. Ask him if he cares about what you've been going through?

Judge
Robinson: That's enough!

Lucifer: How can he say he loves you and stand there silently and watch you suffer? (Turning to Jesus) You've forsaken her and you said you'd never do that! (Turning back to Linda) If I were you, Linda, I'd curse him and die!!

The auditorium was packed with thousands of people. During this particular scene, the whole room went completely silent. In ministry school, I was taught to follow the silence. When the crowd gets quiet, either they are bored or they are engaged.

From the looks of the crowd, they were completely engaged! Many of them told me afterward, how this play ministered to them and how this scene, in particular, was so riveting. It was as if they were on trial and Satan was talking to them.

Others said it represents an ongoing conversation and battle they have been having with Satan for years. I knew then, I was not the only one who felt disappointed and had not had a clear understanding of the prosperity message.

When you are a part of a ministry that majors on the prosperity message, but all they teach are the Biblical principles of prosperity they are giving you only half of what is needed to win the battle. It is like giving you a gun with no bullets or giving you the bullets with no gun. Either way, you look at it, you are not fully equipped to fight. You will be defeated if you do not get the rest of what is needed.

If you are a pastor who teaches the Biblical or spiritual principles of prosperity, it is important that you have programs or ministries in your church that teach members the natural principles of financial increase. You really should not teach one without teaching the other.

The truth is, most people do not understand how money works, moves and multiplies. Most people in the church do not know how to successfully operate and run a business. Most people do not understand marketing, networking, and promoting their businesses, gifts, and talents.

Some do not even know how much to charge or if they should charge at all, for the services they provide. Yet, many pastors do understand these things. This is why their ministries and business are successful, but they have failed to share this information with their congregations. This is one of the main reasons we see prosperity in the pulpit and not in the pews.

> **REASON 9**
>
> **Wealth stays in the pulpit and seldom reaches the pews because... we do not understand business and how to operate a business successfully.**

God has not let us down. He has opened the windows of Heaven over His people. He has given us gifts, talents, witty inventions, concepts, ideas, favor, and businesses, but we have no clue what to do with what He's given us and how to profit from them. The frustration many Christians are facing is not God's fault it is due to a lack of knowledge.

Hosea 4:6 says :

my people are destroyed for lack of knowledge: because thou hast rejected knowledge...

See, we, in the Body of Christ have absorbed all the spiritual knowledge we can possibly get. We know every Scripture in Greek and Hebrew; yet, we have rejected the knowledge the world has on making money. We live in the information age, through the power of the internet and books we can do almost anything we want to do with success and with excellence. Remember, the Scripture says, *the natural is first then the spiritual.* We have been doing things backward and expecting to move forward and we are stuck.

Now, you can argue this point and continue to sit on your sofa, eating potato chips saying "money cometh to me now" all you want, but you'll be 500 pounds and hoarse before money will ever come to you. I understand faith and the power of a faith confession. I know that Hebrews 11:3 says basically that things start out in the spiritual realm and then manifest in the natural realm. On the contrary, I also understand that money is a natural resource, and that it is acquired through a natural process that Christians have to honor and respect.

In Matthew 17:27, when Jesus and Peter had to pay their taxes, Jesus did not call money down from Heaven or silver and gold to come to him now! Jesus is God. He could have very well called the money and it would have come to Him instantly. But Jesus was not operating as God, He was operating as a man and he had to submit to the natural system of acquiring money that was in place.

Jesus told Peter to go to work (at that time Peter's job was a fisherman) and to take the money out of the fish's mouth and pay their taxes. We have to realize when it comes to attracting wealth, doing natural things are first then the spiritual.

We wonder why people like Oprah Winfrey progress in the natural. Then, she works a spiritual principle, such as the law of sowing and reaping by giving away a million dollars and her businesses experience supernatural increase. Why? Because she did the natural things first and then incorporated the spiritual principles.

Did you know Bill Gates, Donald Trump, Warren Buffet, and many other celebrities and professional athletes give away millions of dollars each year? This is one of the reasons they stay rich. They are working a spiritual principle and some of them are not even saved!

They prosper because sowing and reaping is not just a principle. It is a law! Just as the law of gravity works automatically when put into motion, the law of sowing and reaping works in the same way.

When I decided to get my life back on track, the first thing I told myself is that I was going to start tithing again. God told me not to give another dime until I renewed my mind. I went to the book store to get some books on spiritual enrichment. God said, "No, don't buy any more Christian books." He led me to the business and money section. Instead of buying the latest Joyce Meyers or Creflo Dollar book, He led me to authors like Dave Ramsey, Dan Kennedy, Robert Kiyosaki, Suze Orman, and Robert Allen. He wanted me to learn about business, investing, and how money works. These authors are multimillionaires not by chance or inheritance but because they understand money and how to make it.

As I began to read their books, the wisdom I needed to advance, came pouring in. I started incorporating some of the natural principles I had learned, in conjunction with the spiritual principles I already knew, and the increase I had been waiting for began to show up.

The blessings God promises in His Word will begin to manifest for you when you find this missing part. God is so awesome! He led me to write this book because He knew that I was not the only one looking up to Heaven asking, "God where are you?" God loves me and He wants Leah Davis to prosper. He also loves you and wants you to prosper too.

> **REASON 10**
>
> Wealth stays in the pulpit and seldom reaches the pews because... we have failed to access the natural knowledge given by secular financial experts on building and attracting wealth.

Christians have got to learn to stop being prejudice. We put up a brick wall on some of the information the world has to offer because we still think money is evil and that we shouldn't be filling our spirits with that *junk*.

The truth is that the *love* of money is the root of all evil and the stuff these financial experts teach is not all junk. The very thing you are rejecting may be the very thing you need to take you to the next level of increase. Just like you can learn from other ministers in the Body of Christ, besides your pastor, you can also learn from some of these secular financial experts.

REASON 11

Wealth stays in the pulpit and seldom reaches the pews because... we we do not understand investing and profit-sharing.

Bill Gates and Donald Trump are intentional millionaires. They are not millionaires, by chance. Russell Simmons did not just stumble upon billions, Diddy isn't showing up in everybody's videos just to be seen and do his little dance. These people are investors.

They understand they do not have to own it all. They may just own a piece of the pie. However, when you continue to acquire several small pieces before you know it, you will have the whole pie! Pay attention to what these celebrities are doing, instead of what they are wearing, what they're driving, and who they're dating.

I recently went to see the movie *Wall Street: Money Never Sleeps* starring Michael Douglas and Josh Brolin. Josh said to be better equipped for his role in the movie he decided to get more information on Wall Street and investing. He was afforded the opportunity to hang out with people like Warren Buffet and other multi-millionaires who have made large profits from the stock market.

By hanging around them he picked up on some of the tricks of the trade. He took $20,000 of his own money and invested it where they instructed him and he made a quarter of a million dollars on his investment in just 4 months! The wealth of the wicked is not only laid up for the righteous, they are telling us how to get it!

Did you know Warren Buffet wrote tons of books on business, money, and investing? If I were you, I would finish reading this book and sprint to the nearest bookstore. I'm just saying...

CHAPTER 7

The Marching Orders

I am going to say something that will astonish you but you have to hear it. Are you ready? Christians spend too much time at church! This is another reason we struggle financially.

REASON 12

Wealth stays in the pulpit and seldom reaches the pews because... we spend too much time perfecting church business instead of our own.

We are working and serving in multiple ministries and doing busy work. When we need to be at home hearing from God, working on our business plans, and taking the time to invest in our ideas. I know we love our pastors, but many pastors have already achieved the level of success that we are trying to get to. While members are cleaning toilets at the church house or working in some ministry of helps, the pastor is at home planning his next business venture, networking with others, closing business deals, negotiating, and gaining more and more wealth.

It is wonderful to have a heart to volunteer at church but don't think that our spiritual service is going to bring us any money in the natural. I am by no means saying not to work in the ministry of helps or volunteer at the church. What I am saying is do it in moderation.

Some people spend more time working at the church than they do in their own homes. Doing this not only affects your prosperity, but it can also affect other areas of your life.

REASON 13

Wealth stays in the pulpit and seldom reaches the pews because... we only have one stream of income. this limits God and our receiving potential.

Most of us work 9-to-5 jobs and have caps on our salaries. The boss is not giving out the kind of promotion and increases God wants us to have. Honestly, some jobs limit our receiving potential.

For example, if a person works a city job with an agreed-upon salary contract, the boss is obligated to pay only what complies with the contract. Perhaps there will be a bonus here and there. There may even be a small percentage annual raise. However, for the most part, the salary is set.

How do we expect God to bless us when we are only giving him one avenue of income to work with?

The blessings that God wants to give to us may very well come through entrepreneurship. This doesn't mean we should all quit our jobs. However, it may mean we need to work a side business to gain extra profit.

I started a side business selling Mary Kay and in three weeks I made $1000! I got the idea from a friend whose 9 to 5 wasn't cutting it, so she started selling Mary Kay for extra income. She has made an extra $3000 per month, consistently for over two years.

I am not saying Mary Kay is the way to the promise land, but I am saying entrepreneurship may well be the way. All that is needed is something to sell, the ability to provide a service, or the willingness to distribute a product.

I know many Christians who have made large profits from multilevel marketing businesses. We simply use our natural gifts and talents and make a business out of them. Everyone cannot act, play an instrument, or sing but perhaps you have excellent administrative skills, are good with children, or are exceptional at cooking or cleaning. Whatever your skills, use them to bring you increase. *Find your niche and let it make you rich!*

We need to have multiple levels of income and increase coming into our lives. This means we have to be willing to do this four-letter word called WORK. This doesn't mean go get a second job with another salary cap.

Take the limits off! We need jobs without glass ceilings. We need a side business where the amount of money that can be made is based solely on our diligence and God's faithfulness. We need to see His favor at work in our lives. We need to experience Him bringing new clients and customers into our circles every day.

When we depend solely upon Him, He will provide for us like never before. He's waiting and He's willing to flood our lives with abundance. We have given, sacrificed, and volunteered long enough! Now it is time to get busy!

CHAPTER 8

The Mandate

I went to a non-denominational church. Some people call such churches *Word* of *Faith* Churches. These types of churches focus more on teaching Biblical principles than on messages that stir emotions. People who go to Word of Faith Churches are consistently taught the principles of faith and prosperity. Members of these ministries definitely learn the Bible and have a good understanding of the Word; however, I have noticed some spiritual arrogance among some of the people, as well as a lack of compassion.

These church members are taught the principles of faith and are trained, not to be ruled by their emotions or the senses. When the storms of life arise, congregants are taught to respond in faith, rather than reacting emotionally.

The Bible tells us we are to *walk by faith and not by sight*. The problem with the message of faith is that sometimes, it is being taught for selfish gain. In my non-denominational church, we were taught…to use our faith to get a car, a house, or a promotion. We were to use our faith to get financial increase in general but many people in these circles have *faith failures* because selfishness is the opposite of love and faith only works *by* and *through* love.

When we sow our seeds, we should do it out of our love for God, not because we are trying to get something from Him. In the Body of Christ, we have to learn to stop giving to get. A lot of times we give because of our need, yet when we give, we must ask ourselves these questions.

1. Am I giving because of my situation and I need God to help me?
2. Am I giving because I believe God's Word concerning sowing and reaping, and my seed is an act of my faith?
3. Am I giving because I love God and His Word, and I trust Him?

Actually, questions 1 & 2 will not work if the motive for giving is not based on question 3. Our seeds cannot move the hand of God. Faith can move God's hand but the motive behind faith must be love.

Many Word of Faith preachers may disagree with the statement, "Love is greater than faith." The Apostle Paul says in **I Corinthians 13:13, And now these three remain faith, hope, and love. But the greatest of these is love.** Many Christians have not received God's promise of prosperity because we have spent too much time mastering faith and have forgotten about love.

REASON 14

Wealth stays in the pulpit and seldom reaches the pews because... we do not understand synergy.

Another aspect of love is sharing and giving to others. Now, sharing doesn't necessarily mean the gift has to come specifically from us. We can provide and create opportunities for others to increase.

There is a thing called *synergy*. Synergy is when two or more agents work together to produce a result not obtainable by any of the agents independently. We need each other. We cannot achieve our goals without each other. Christians need to support, help, and be committed to making each other prosper. Synergy says we cannot do this as independent agents. We must band together to achieve a common goal.

Our commitments do not always have to be financial. They may be referential. Small gestures, such as making a phone call, sending an email, or words of endorsement, can be a blessing to others and bring them increase.

I am sure each of us can think of someone right now we can help to prosper. We may know someone who needs a particular gift, talent, or service and can connect the one in need to the one who has or is the resource. Yet, we sit, saying nothing and holding up another person's blessings and ultimately holding up our own blessings. We have to stop being selfish and learn to love!

One reason God wants to prosperous us is so we can love on others and be a blessing to them. God tells Abraham, "I'm going to bless you so that you can be a blessing, and in you shall all the families of the earth be blessed." God may not bless us with material wealth and blessings if we are not willing to share it. Our faith may not work if we drop the ball where love is concerned. We can make all the faith confessions we want, sow till our fingers fall off and we will still be as *broke as the Ten Commandments* until we perfect our love walk!

Another issue I have is that some preachers think they own the members who are a part of their congregations and try to control them as if they are puppets on a string. For example, I am a playwright, screenwriter, songwriter, etc. My gifts are for the Body of Christ, not just for the church I attend. If I write a play about healing and Bishop *so and so,* down the street, wants to pay me to share my gift with his congregation, this should not be a problem. Yet, some preachers have a major issue with this.

Many Christians believe God for their gifts to make room for them and to take them to new levels of prosperity. However, their pastors are interfering and blocking their blessings. This whole mindset is based on fear, not faith, and has no attribute of love whatsoever.

Instead of letting the members flourish and receive financial increase from other sources, pastors covet their gifts for themselves. This is a common practice among many churches. They prostitute and exploit people's gifts and talents, thinking they are saving the ministry money. Instead, they are putting God's people in bondage. This is not love and, sadly, many preachers are operating their ministries in this way!

I have seen anointed ministers turn down invitations to preach at other churches because their pastors did not approve of this. There have also been instances where the pastor allowed the minister to go minister, but only if the church he/she was going to would make the check out to him (the pastor) and not to the minister who actually did the speaking.

I understand that there is a code of honor that associate ministers/pastors have for their senior pastors. Oftentimes senior pastors only want their associate ministers to preach and serve at the church that they are employed by or represent. Senior pastors also require that these ministers ask approval before they do any preaching and teaching outside of their church body. This code is not Biblical, but it is still implemented by many ministries in the Body of Christ.

All ministers' allegiance should be first to God. We should respect our senior pastors, but not allow them to put us into bondage. Christians have to realize that there is a difference between being a servant and a slave. If senior pastors want their ministers to only serve their particular church body, then they should be sure that they cover these ministers both spiritually and financially.

I know of a minister of music whose pastor truly covers her both spiritually and financially. She is quite popular and often gets invitations to minister all over the country. Her pastor does not forbid her to accept these invitations. She accepts them at her leisure because the financial needs for her and her family are already met by the ministry.

It is unfair when senior pastors live leagues above their ministerial staff. The truth is the ministerial staff has more hands-on contact with the members of the church. In mega church settings, the associate ministers/pastors are the ones that handle the counseling sessions, family problems, hospital visits, funerals, weddings, etc. These ministers should be fairly compensated for the work that they perform. It's sad to say in some churches, this is not the case.

It is timeout for preachers thinking they can take ownership of God's people and treat them like slaves! Loose the saints and let them go do what God has called and equipped them to do! God is watching and taking note of how His people are being treated and how some pastors are offending and scattering the sheep. How can preachers honestly say they love God's people and continue attempting to control them and keep them from prospering?

From what Biblical principle does this type of logic stem? The truth is this rule comes from the heart of man and not from God. Jesus said, "Go ye into all the world and preach the gospel"... If the message being preached is the Good News of Jesus Christ, ministers are not limited to one body of believers. We have a mandate from Jesus Christ to take the message to all the world!

With all of my frustration in working in ministry and all the things I have experienced, there are many things too painful to mention. Many of these hurts came at the hands of people proclaiming to be Christians. I still have to forgive them. If I want a clear path so that the blessings can flow in my life, I have to get rid of unforgiveness.

Unforgiveness is a MAJOR blessing blocker. We cannot expect God to forgive us of our sins if we do not forgive the people who have offended us. How can we receive God's best while still holding hatred in our hearts? In fact, the Bible urges us not to even give offerings when we have not forgiven our neighbors.

Matthews 5:21

If you enter your place of worship and, about to make an offering, you suddenly remember a grudge a friend has against you, abandon your offering, leave immediately, go to this friend and make things right. Then and only then, come back and work things out with God.

I know this is hard. There have been some people in my life that have hurt me, but I had to let it go and forgive them. No matter how badly they treated me or how much it hurt, I had to do what God's Word says and walk in forgiveness. So let's suck it up and do what we know we have to do! No one is worth causing us to miss out on God's blessings.

CHAPTER 9

The Master

Got a question for you… Does God want his children to prosper? The answer to this question may seem simple to you, but people have been battling with this question for years. If you want to know God's plan for mankind, in regards to prosperity, we must go back to the first man and the state and conditions in which he lived in the Garden of Eden.

God gave Adam and Eve everything that they could possibly have ever wanted, needed, or desired in the garden. They had an abundance of food to eat, cool springs of water to drink, a beautiful dwelling place filled with beautiful scenery. They were clothed in the glory of God. They had purpose, they had each other and they had constant open fellowship with God. Their lives were perfect!

Since this is the state and conditions God chose for the first man, it is safe to say God wishes that all mankind live a life free of care and concern, filled with abundance, purpose, good health, and total dependence upon Him. This theme rings true throughout the Scriptures. From Genesis to Revelation, we see God wants His people to be prosperous. Now the God-kind of prosperity is not just about money, wealth, and riches. Scripture indicates, when God speaks of prosperity, He means *total life prosperity*. He wants us to prosper in our hearts, minds, families, health, businesses, emotions, relationships, and our finances.

III John 2:

"Beloved, I wish above all things that thou mayest prosper and be in health, even as thy soul prospereth".

St. John 10:10:

"The thief cometh not, but for to steal, and to kill, and to destroy: I am come that they might have life, and that they might have it more abundantly".

So we see God's definition of prosperity and man's definition of prosperity are very different. Can it be that our motives for having prosperity and God's motives for wanting us to prosper are different as well?

He wants us to give Him the glory and honor when He blesses us. This may cause people who do not know Him to *want* to know Him. God's motive is always to draw others into Him and into His

Kingdom. The reason God sent Jesus is to seek and to save those who are lost. God loves people and perhaps one reason God has allowed the message of prosperity in the Bible is so that we can continue His work by drawing others to Him, through love and charity.

Everyone is not called to the fivefold ministries, so we are not necessarily going out into the world preaching and teaching the gospel. As laypersons, we are to be a light to the world and to support those who are sent to preach the gospel. God loves us and can multiply our finances but our money has a dual purpose.

Our wealth, riches, and increase are for us to give into works that will bring more people into the kingdom of God AND for us to have a good life here on the Earth. It is not merely for us to lavish ourselves with material items and selfishly heap up treasures for ourselves and our children.

2 Corinthians 9:8:

And God is able to make all grace (every favor and earthly blessing) come to you in abundance, so that you may always and under all circumstances and whatever the need be self-sufficient [possessing enough to require no aid or support and furnished in abundance for every good work and charitable donation].

We can see from Corinthians that God wants us in position to give into good works and charitable donations. As believers, one of the good works we are supposed to be involved in is the spreading of the Good News of Jesus Christ. We should be connected to ministries that are implementing outreach ministries, mission projects, and coming up with creative ways to bring the lost and hurting into the Kingdom of God.

By our own observations, we can determine if our local church is doing its part to win the loss. We should give offerings accordingly. Our giving does not always have to be to a church. We should give and support any organization involved in helping people and spreading the goodness of Jesus.

> **REASON 15**
>
> Wealth stays in the pulpit and seldom reaches the pews because... we do not know our God-given purpose and the resources needed to fulfill that purpose.

Now, let's talk about purpose for a minute. I believe that God has a specific reason for our existence and that everyone's life has purpose. It is up to us to search the heart of God to identify our purpose in His kingdom and I'm convinced that our gifts and talents are linked to our purpose. Once you have identified and are walking in your God-given purpose, I believe that God will bless you with the resources you need to fulfill that purpose.

Now, everybody doesn't need a million dollars to fulfill their purpose. This is not to say that God won't bless you with over and above because He is a gracious God. I am saying that according to Philippians 4:19, you have a for a sure promise, that God will supply your needs.

Through all of the frustration I was experiencing, God always supplied my needs but I wasn't excited about Him supplying my needs. I wanted the wealth, riches, and abundance that the pastor was so hyped about, but was it just hype? Did God really promise me millions, a mansion and a Mercedes?

Sometimes we read stories in the Bible and we see where God has blessed someone with abundance and we want to demand and command God to bless us in like manner. We never think that the blessings they received were specific for their time, their season, and their purpose. Solomon was a billionaire. His God-given purpose was to rebuild the temple, which required him to have an abundance of financial resources. His riches were specific to his purpose.

Do you know your purpose? Most importantly, do you know what's needed to fulfill your God-given purpose? You might be gifted at making people feel welcomed and received. Your God-given purpose might be, to be, a greeter in the church. Here you are calling down the blessings of Abraham, the favor of Ruth, and the wisdom of Job, and your purpose in the Kingdom does not require you to have what they had. It is true that God is no respecter of persons, but every person has a purpose, and the resources needed to fulfill that purpose may differ.

If you desire to be a millionaire and your purpose in His kingdom doesn't require a million-dollar flow, then you must be more aggressive at working the natural principles that attract wealth. You may have to work harder, invest or execute some type of business venture to achieve this, but it is possible.

We just have to make sure our hearts and motives are right when it comes to money. When God blesses us, we should continue to support His Kingdom and give Him the glory.

REASON 16

Wealth stays in the pulpit and seldom reaches the pews because... we do not listen when God speaks to us about opportunities that can bring us increase.

Proverbs 3:5 says:

Lean on, trust in, and be confident in the Lord with all your heart and mind and do not rely on your own insight or understanding. In all your ways know, recognize, and acknowledge Him, and He will direct and make straight and plain your paths.

Another way God proves He wants us to prosper is that God will talk to us concerning giving and business opportunities. God wants to be involved in every area of our lives. He eagerly and patiently waits for us to let Him in so He can show us the way and so that we can give Him the glory.

I have to say I learned this the hard way. I remember doing research to help my brother jump-start his real estate business. I would find properties for sale so he could buy them, make repairs and rent them out.

I came across this one property that was in horrible condition. It was a duplex, located in the lower ninth ward in New Orleans. The windows and doors were gone, the roof was damaged, the floor had collapsed and the grass around the house was taller than me! The owner was selling it dirt cheap. He just wanted to get rid of it. He inherited the property after his mother died and no one in his family wanted it.

I brought the property to my brother's attention. He said, "There is no way I am buying that piece of trash."

I heard God say as clear as day, "*You buy it.*" I wondered if God was serious. I thought, *God you want me to buy that hunk of junk?*

He spoke to me again and said the same thing: *"You buy it."*

I had just sold my condo, my credit was good and I had no debt. I found a bank that agreed to make me a small loan to purchase this prosperity.

I kept wondering why God wanted me to buy such damaged goods. I began to lean on my own understanding, wondering how I was going to fix this place up. I knew nothing about construction or carpentry. I also wondered how much it would cost to repair this house. I guessed, by the looks of the house that it would take at least $30,000.

I just kept toiling in my mind, wasting time and failing to do what God said. I even went to my brother and told him I was planning on buying the property and he told me I was crazy.

God spoke again, but this time it was with more instructions. God said, *"Buy it and insure it."*

I did not listen and it cost me big time! The house was only $13,000. It would have cost me only a few hundred dollars to insure it. God spoke to me in June of 2005. Hurricane Katrina came in August 2005. The place where the house was located was completely destroyed. Katrina washed the whole house away. Nothing was left, not even the slab.

If I had bought it and insured the property, I could have gotten around $100,000 from the insurance policy. I would have also received grant money from FEMA. Additionally, the property was on the last street of the lower ninth ward and the first street in Chalmette, LA which means, it would have been affected by the oil spill that happened in Chalmette as the result of Katrina. There was a multimillion-dollar class-action lawsuit that I would have been eligible to participate in. Although the house was in poor condition, it was in the perfect location for me to gain financially.

While I was worried about how I was going to get the money to fix the house up, God already knew Katrina was gonna tear it down. God was setting me up for a wealth transfer and I didn't know it.

What is God setting up for you that you are still fighting?

If I could turn back the hands of time and get that moment back, you know I would buy every house on that block! God is not obligated to give me that moment back. That transfer of wealth was meant for that season alone and once it's gone, it's gone.

I am sad to say that every day that I was broke following Hurricane Katrina was not God's fault. It was mine. He had already planned out my future. He knew Katrina was coming and He had my provision ready. All I had to do was listen to His instructions.

He still took great care of me and my family after the storm but He wanted to do more, so much more. He wanted to *show off* in me. He knew I would have told everybody: "*Look what the Lord has done!*" He wanted this to be my testimony of His goodness to draw others to Him.

I hope God is speaking to you as you read this. I hope He's revealing to you what He is setting up in your life. God wants us to prosper, and if we are sensitive to His voice He will tell us where the wealth is.

Do not do as I did. Don't try to figure God out. He's so much smarter than us. We are so prideful that sometimes we think we know more than Him. Mary says it best at the wedding before Jesus performed His first miracle, she said, "*Whatever He tells you to do, do it.*" Take Mary's advice.

CHAPTER 10

The Move

Greed is attempting to get something for nothing, to take without exchange.

Some may say some prosperity teachers are greedy. I beg to differ, based on the definition of greed. When we go to church, what do we get in return? We met the greeters at the door. The ushers showed us to our seats. The choir sang. The preacher gave us revelation knowledge and inspired us. We went home feeling good and encouraged. So, we actually did not get something for nothing. We received a very pleasant experience.

If we paid our tithes and offerings, then we contributed to this experience. Generally, our tithes and offerings go toward the expenses of the church. So in essence, *we got what we paid for.* If we did not tithe, we got what *somebody else paid for*. Based on the definition of greed and this example, the non-tithers are the ones who are greedy!

I have got a question for you…Do you think it is the pastor's job to improve the quality of your life? It is both Godly and right for them to teach messages and create lessons that can improve our lives if we follow the teachings. However, it is not their job to make sure we prosper.

In a perfect world, pastors would be available to show us individually, what we need to do to walk in the manifestation of God's promise of prosperity. They would be there to greet us each morning, to pray and agree with us, help us make our daily confessions, set up our daily agenda, help promote and market our businesses, tell us who to call, what to say, and help us make and close business deals.

We all know this is not going to happen nor should we place such high expectations on our pastors. There is someone who <u>can</u> do all of the things listed above, with each of us, every single day and He is the Holy Spirit.

Isaiah 48:17 says:

Thus saith the LORD, thy Redeemer,
the Holy One of Israel; I am the LORD thy God
which teacheth thee to profit, which leadeth thee by
the way that thou shouldest go.

We have help from Heaven. We simply have to learn to tap into our heavenly resources and access the power to get wealth. It would be great if our churches provided us with both the spiritual and natural elements to help us prosper. However, this is not the preacher's job. Their assignment is to teach us spiritual things.

If we never pick up our Bibles, get on our knees to pray, open up our mouths to confess God's Word, tithe, or give an offering, it is not on them. Preachers lose no sleep when we decide not to act on God's Word. They will keep teaching us 'til we get it. Until then, we are on our own!

REASON 17

Wealth stays in the pulpit and seldom reaches the pews because... Christians have failed to realize we are responsible for our own prosperity.

My primary purpose for writing this book is to let believers know we must take responsibility for our own prosperity. If we do not receive the promised blessings of God, it is not God's fault nor is it the preacher's fault. The fault is our own!

We must come to realize our pastors do not have all the answers and we should not expect them to. They may not have the money or the vision to implement all the special programs and ministries that will help us advance and grow financially. If they do not, we must take responsibility and get the information and the knowledge we need for ourselves.

As more pastors get caught up in sin and churches begin to shut down, we have to realize we are in a day when our dependency must be totally on God. This is okay because God + you = a majority. I heard someone say the reason miracles are happening in third world countries and not in America, is because we have options. In third world countries, people either trust God or die!

We may not always have 20,000 member churches and 100,000 square foot buildings. We have to know God's Word for ourselves and have a personal, intimate relationship with God ourselves. We have to learn to access God and get what we need from Him with or without our spouses, with or without our prayer partners, with or without our jobs, with or without our churches, and with or without our pastors. We can't keep counting on others for revelation and instruction. We need to know *what* to do, *when* to do it, *how* we should do it and *why* we are doing it, for ourselves!

CHAPTER 11

The Moral Standard

Now I have said a lot of things about preachers in this book but I am in no wise against preachers. I know that there are some awesome anointed preachers in the Body of Christ who do not have an obsession with money. Recently, a pastor told his congregation not to give their tithe to the church but to give it to somebody whom they know is presently having trouble financially.

I know of a pastor, after hurricane Katrina, who filled a bucket with money and gave each family in his church a hundred dollars, as a token of love and support. I was recently in a service where the pastor asked the members of his congregation who were unemployed to stand, and he told them he would pay their bills for that month.

These kind, unselfish acts came at the hands of preachers who have a heart for God's people. I do not believe that all preachers are selfish nor do I believe that all of the preachers and teachers of prosperity have ill motives and hidden agendas.

You know what I believe, and this is just my opinion? I believe some preachers are afraid of going back to being broke. They may have come from rags to riches and are afraid of going backward. Although they command us to walk by faith, *they* are not walking by faith. When their expenses become overwhelming, they look to us to meet their needs, instead of God.

I also believe some pastors are so addicted to their lavish lifestyles that the condition of their hearts changes and they no longer love God's people the way that they should. They begin to value their money more than their members.

For example, some pastors have stipulations on helping their members when they have a need. If the members are not tithers they are refused aid or benevolence based on their giving reports. As I recall, before Jesus performed a miracle, He didn't have the disciples check their giving reports or asked the person to give Him an offering before He helped them. The Bible says because Jesus was moved with compassion, He healed them.

I remember a young lady who was an exotic dancer but became a waitress after giving her life to Christ. Her monthly income changed dramatically because of her lifestyle change. She went to the church for help with her rent and the pastor told her, "The church is not going to help you with your rent. You have to use your faith to get your rent paid."

She had been saved less than a month. She knew very little about faith or how to use it to get her needs met. Ironically, she did exactly what he told her to do, she used what she had faith in to get her rent paid and went back to dancing at the club and left the church.

Some pastors in the body of Christ are so self-centered and money-hungry that they recklessly operate their ministries, making decisions that can be harmful to the people God has placed in their lives. It is shameful when pastors have full-time employees but refuse to pay for medical, dental, and unemployment benefits because it saves the church money. As an employee, if you get sick and have to be hospitalized, you not only have to deal with the emotional and physical stress of the illness, you also have to bare the weight of medical expenses.

It is hard to believe that on days when the offerings are expected to be large, pastors place security guards with armed rifles in the service and have the ushers carry concealed weapons. The members of the church could potentially lose their lives if there is an incident and someone one attempts to steal the tithes.

I believe the reason we often get so offended by pastors is that we see them in the wrong light. When we think of the fivefold ministry gifts, we think of them as spiritually sound, morally righteous, honest, faithful, loving, caring, and compassionate. Yet, when pastors make mistakes, bad judgments, foolish decisions, are rude, unmannerly, arrogant, or fall into sin, we are devastated because we have had them on such a high pedestal.

Throughout my life, I have come to understand one thing… pastors are first and for most businessmen. They are the CEOs of their ministries and run them as such. Yes, they are men of God and have a calling from God on their lives but just in case you haven't noticed, the church is no longer brick and mortar. The 21st-century church is a business!

Most CEOs and business owners have a commitment to themselves, their families, shareholders, investors, employees, and customers to obtain the greatest profits possible so that they can stay in business and be able to honor their commitments. To settle for anything less shows a lack of responsibility, integrity and can leave the business vulnerable and in danger of folding. Preachers are no different and believe it or not, they think the same way.

I was once in a meeting and the preacher said when the church is going through a tough time financially, the strategy to get them out of a financial hole is to host a conference. I cannot fault him for being a brilliant businessman, who knew how to keep his company afloat. However, I can say that his motive for having a conference was not to give spiritual enrichment to its attendees. It was to make money!

Is this wrong or, right? He has an obligation to his church, his family, and his employees to keep his business (which just happens to be a church) up and running. If it was Bill Gates and he hosted an event that he knew would bring in a lot of money to Microsoft, would we question his integrity as a businessman? Yet, we think there is a difference between selling computer software and preaching the Gospel, which is free and already purchased by the blood of Jesus?

When pastors are faced with tough economic times, such as we are having now, and have to think of ways to make money for the ministry and use things like conferences and seminars to do so, are they operating out of faith or fear? Are they depending on God's power to get wealth or their own power?

This is why we must use discernment when we go to these events. Only God knows the real motive and reasons a particular event is being held in the first place. We have to determine if we are getting an experience or an empowerment. Is revelation and an impartation from the Holy Ghost taking place? Is God there? The tricky part to this is, the Bible says in **Matthew 18:20:** *For where*

two or three are gathered together in my name, there am I in the midst of them.

God is going to show up because His people are gathered together in His name. Most preachers know this is true and perhaps this justifies their motives… God showed up and the people were blessed.

God does show up but He doesn't always stay. I have been in conferences where it was obvious the presence of God was there and moments later it was even more obvious He had left the building! This was especially true once the real motives behind the gathering began to become apparent.

I remember being at a conference where they had *express sales*. The ushers walked the aisles, with bags filled with books, CD series; t-shirts, etc. They sold these items to the attendees during the conference. The benefit was that participants did not have to stand in long lines after service. We were able to buy what was needed from our seats.

This went on throughout the entire service… after praise and worship, announcements, soloist, exhortations, testimonies, etc. They always made a product to offer and had an express sale.

I recall how frustrating it was to be in service for over two hours and the main speaker still had not been introduced because, at every break in the service, something was being promoted from the pulpit that involved a money transaction. I felt they had invited all these people to come to the conference just to make money!

> **REASON 18:** Wealth stays in the pulpit and seldom reaches the pews because... Christians think when they are inside the four walls of the church they are in a safe place and cannot be taken advantage of.

It also troubles me when preachers say things like, "If you give a thousand dollars right now, God is going to bless you!" What if you don't have a thousand dollars right then? Is God going to say, "Talk to the hand and holla at me when you get the money?" This would make God a respecter of persons and the Bible clearly says that He is not a respecter of persons. This is not an attribute of His character. Many times preachers make statements like this just to raise money.

Preachers do not rationalize the implications of the possible outcomes. For example, if God did not say to give a certain amount and people give their money and do not receive the blessing, healing, increase, breakthrough, etc. that was promised, some people may begin to doubt God. The people who do not have the money to give (due to their downturned financial status), may think they do not qualify for a blessing. It is so important that we know how to hear from God. People are being deceived, living in the moment, looking at their needs, not having heard God say to give anything.

Preachers must be careful that their corporate responsibilities do not override their moral and spiritual obligations. I understand preachers are under a lot of pressure and scrutiny; however, some may have known about the pressures when they accepted the call to ministry. Preachers are expected to live holy, moral, and righteous lives and to operate with integrity. Just as water comes with the wet, the fivefold ministry comes with a standard of righteousness and excellence. I understand preachers are not perfect and they make mistakes, yet their mistakes affect others. They affect the body of believers who have been placed under their care and influence the entire Body of Christ as a whole.

We do not care what the owners of fortune 500 companies do morally or ethically because it does not affect our faith. Do we care that some billionaires get a new wife every three years, that many have multiple children out of wedlock, or that some successful business owners are drug addicts? Yet, when a nationally acclaimed minister gets accused of performing homosexual acts with young males, you better believe it makes Christians around the world cringe.

Preachers, I understand you have bills, budgets, and bottom lines that you have to consider, but you do not have to squander money and scheme your members to honor your financial commitments. Your commitment to God, His Word, and His people should be greater than any of your obligations! If you stay committed to God, God will stay committed to you, and in times of economic hardships, you will prevail because you chose to trust in God and God alone!

To make this an even playing field, I can't just get on the people in the pulpit (about their moral standards), and not take it to the folks in the pews. We too have been commanded by God to be holy and walk in integrity. I know some Christians who are obtaining wealth by questionable means. The same Spirit that raised Jesus from the dead dwells in us. God can lift us up out of poverty without us doing anything illegal, unlawful and unrighteous.

We do not have to do what the world does to obtain wealth and riches. We operate under a different system and a different set of rules. We are children of the King. King's kids do not go outside of the Kingdom when there is a need. King's kids go to the Father and He supplies it. So, why do we feel we need to operate outside of the Kingdom when we have a need, when our Father, the King of Kings, is ready and willing to help us!

Are we aware God is watching? Though we may be squandering and scheming to drive that Benz, that BMW or to live in that gated community is it really worth losing our souls? Integrity means everything, to Christians. People are always looking for something real.

Some sinners may be as fake as a three-dollar bill but they are always testing and poking at Christians to see if we are real. Let the world see that Jesus is not only real, He is real in us! Let the love of God that has been shed abroad in our hearts begin to spread to others.

We, as Christians, cannot be cold and heartless, backstabbing and cut throat like people that are in the world. We should handle our business affairs, relationships, and transactions differently. Let integrity be our guide.

CHAPTER 12

The Mistakes

Ephesians 2:10:

For we are God's [own] handiwork (His workmanship), recreated in Christ Jesus, [born anew] that we may do those good works which God predestined (planned beforehand) for us [taking paths which He prepared ahead of time], that we should walk in them [living the good life which He prearranged and made ready for us to live].

God wants us to live the good life, filled with His very best. There are mistakes we make that keep us separated from the blessings He wishes to bestow upon us. I recently heard a song that says, "You can't win still living in sin." I thought to myself, *Wow, the songwriter is right on when he wrote this song!*

Now the Bible tells us in **Romans 3:23: For all have sinned and come short of the glory of God.** This means no person on earth has not sinned in his or her lifetime. In fact, the Bible tells us we are born into sin. This is why we must be born again. Once a person has accepted Jesus Christ as Lord and Savior, this does not mean the person will never sin again. It means Jesus took away our sins and makes us the righteousness of God.

Since we are His righteousness, we should do righteous deeds. However, the manifestation of this only comes through the renewing of the mind.

3 John 2 says:

Beloved, I wish above all things that thou mayest prosper and be in health, even as thy soul prospereth.

Basically, this Scripture is saying we will prosper in our everyday affairs and maintain good health when our minds are renewed. For example, if we continue to eat fast food, junk food, and things that are bad for our bodies, we will never have good health. We will not have good health until we change our minds about our diets.

The same is true when it comes to sin. We will never experience all that God has in store for us until we change our minds about the sin we are currently engaging in. We all know that no sin is greater than another in God's eyes. We know what challenges we have with certain sins. I admonish each of us to make the necessary changes so that we can be in position for increase. No sin is worth missing out on what God has for us.

Sin is a major barrier that can keep supernatural increase from us. Notice I said *supernatural* increase and not *natural* increase.

There are many sinners in the world who are wealthy. They have done the natural things to attract wealth, riches and increase to their lives. Simply because they have financial prosperity does not mean they have total life prosperity. We have seen it too many times, how rich and famous people have so many relationship problems, family problems, health issues, emotional baggage, drug addictions, sex addictions, depression, and sometimes even commit suicide. This is because their father, who is the devil, only gave them one piece of the pie, which is financial prosperity. Yet, the total life prosperity, for which they long for, can only be found in Jesus Christ.

As believers, we, too, can do natural things to experience increase without living holy lives, but God has a special endowment of blessings He wishes to bestow upon us if we will eliminate sin from our lives.

Jeremiah 5:25:

Your iniquities have turned these blessings away, and your sins have kept good [harvests] from you.

Notice the text doesn't just say, "*harvest*." It says, "...*good harvest*." This means we can have a harvest, but some of the crops may be rotten, spoiled, bitter, or infested with bugs and pestilence. God says we will receive a *good* harvest when we do away with sin.

I noticed in my own life when I decided to live a holy life, pleasing in God's eyes, His blessings flowed to me more rapidly and more easily. Sometimes, we have to realize the greater good in our situation and eliminate the distractions in our lives. To receive our good harvest, we may have to disconnect from people we love and care about. Once we realize that what God has for us is greater than that relationship or addiction, God can flood our lives with increase.

Another mistake we often make is in our speech. If you have ever heard the prosperity message, you know part of the message is about *speaking in line with God's Word*. Despite the circumstances, God's Word is true. We should always agree with what His Word says about us, rather than agreeing with what our situation is telling us.

Sometimes, we forget words are seeds. When we speak negatively, we are sowing a harvest filled with negativity, into our lives.

For example, if your bank account is low and one of your children asks for money and you reply, "I ain't got no money. I'm broke." You have just sown seeds of lack and insufficiency in your own life. Perhaps you will say, "I only spoke the truth. Do you want me to lie?" No, I want you to speak the truth.

God's Word is Truth. God says He will supply all our needs and we are blessed and empowered to prosper. So, all we need to do is agree with what God says. When believing God for increase, our walk, our talk, our feet, and hands must be moving simultaneously, in one direction… towards our destiny.

REASON 19

Wealth stays in the pulpit and seldom reaches the pews because... we devalue our gifts, talents, and services and give them away for free or at a discount.

One of the biggest mistakes we make when it comes to getting the wealth to flow into our lives is in the area of our self-esteem. We may feel we are not worthy of the best because of the following reasons: our socio-economic status, ethnicity, or educational background.

I am not just talking about seeing ourselves as God sees us or about feeling as if we do not deserve to be rich. I am talking about not valuing ourselves for who we are, what we do, and demanding the best for our gifts and talents.

Sometimes we exploit our own gifts by not charging what we should for the services we provide. I am not talking about price gouging, hoarding, unfair rates and not having integrity. I am talking about thinking our gifts, talents or the services we provide are worthy of the fair market value.

Perhaps some of us are novices. Perhaps the business we own is new. We may be inexperienced, so we cheat ourselves. One person may not have as much experience or education as another, yet maybe anointed in a particular area and may display more excellence than people who call themselves the professionals in that particular field.

I once had a writing deal with E. Perry. I know you are wondering, "Who the heck is E. Perry?" Well E. Perry is Tyler Perry's brother... well at least this is what he told me. He wanted to break into the gospel stage play industry, but he was not a writer. He read one of my scripts and wanted to launch his career using a play that I wrote.

Even though I wrote the entire script and the songs, he only offered me 40¢ per ticket. His reasoning was, "I have the Perry name and my brother is going to endorse me. This means that my shows will sell out like his shows, so you are actually getting a good deal since you are an unknown playwright."

My response was, "You may have the Perry name but your first name is not Tyler. Even if he decides to endorse the show, 40¢ per ticket is unfair to me as the playwright, especially when the tickets start at $35 a seat."

After a series of negotiations, this deal fell through. I would not back down and allow him to prostitute my gifts!

God gives us gifts and talents to bring us increase. When we give them at a discount, we are only cheating ourselves. We should feel as if we are the best at what we do and no one can do it better. No one is going to pay for something the seller deems as worthless.

REASON 20

Wealth stays in the pulpit and seldom reaches the pews because... we don't understand that people will pay for the things they really want.

Coach sells their bags for $300. If you want a Coach bag, you better have $300 plus tax to take it out of the store. As many times as I have been in the Coach store, I have never seen anyone dispute the prices. People simply take out their credit cards and pay with a smile, because this is *the* bag they want.

About two years ago, a friend and I were in the mall. It just happened to be the day Apple came out with their new iPhone 12. These phones were selling for more than $1000 a piece and the line to get one extended outside of the store and around the corner.

It does not matter if we are in a recession, pandemic, or whatever. People will pay for what they really want.

We do not need to have a large company such as Apple or Coach backing us for people to want our products and services. We have the name of Jesus backing us. As long as the service we provide is good and we walk in integrity in our businesses, we do not have to shortchange ourselves. If someone wants what you have, they will pay the price. If they think it is too much and will not pay, perhaps you are marketing to the wrong consumer!

> **REASON 21**
>
> Wealth stays in the pulpit and seldom reaches the pews because... we are doing business with people who are on our level instead of going to where the money is.

I know a lady who lives in the "hood" but she provides a service to affluent clients in an upscale area in Houston. She knows that the people in the "hood" would not dare pay her asking prices so she set up her business in and around the people she knows have no problem paying them.

She knows God has given her this business so that she can prosper. She does extremely well because she places value on what she does and won't settle for less.

REASON 22

Wealth stays in the pulpit and seldom reaches the pews because... we don't charge the industry standard for our services when we are doing business with churches.

I have another question for you. Why do we feel when we provide a service or share our gifts or talents in the church that we must do so at a discount? I have seen so many Christians short change themselves when they are doing work for the church. I know you are saying, "But that is my pastor and I have to show him favor."

My question to you is... "When are you going to begin thinking like a business person?" Your pastors think like people who are in business. He knows as the pastor, he can get your product or service for free or at a discount, and believe me he banks on it. In your mind, you are doing something spiritual and, in his mind, he just saved his business lots of money.

We have to learn to separate the natural from spiritual. Business is Business. When we give tithes and offerings to the church this is spiritual. Our businesses are altogether different and should be separate. Perhaps we do not understand this, but pastors do.

When a pastor goes to Walmart, does he get a discount because he is a pastor? Does the cashier say, "You are a man of God. You preach the Word. You lay hands on the sick. You change lives, so I am going to give you 75% off your purchase." Walmart is a business and the pastor knows when he walks into Walmart, he must pay full price. In fact, he expects this!

There is nothing wrong with giving or sowing our services into the ministry but at least be smart about it. Let's say you have an office supply business. You can charge the church the regular price so they can purchase their supplies throughout the year. However, when the church is giving out school supplies for a back to school event, by all means, donate some supplies to the church. The kids benefit, the ministry saves money and you get a tax write off.

Let's say you have a catering business and the church wants you to cater an event. Charge a fair market price for the food and labor and throw in some extra veggies, meat, or desserts. Maybe you can even make the pastor something special, like a big juicy t-bone steak. The bottom line is, get your money!

I know you're saying, "Dang, Leah, that's pretty harsh!" If they can afford $300,000 cars and 20,000 square foot homes, helicopters, and private jets, then they can afford to pay you for your products, services, gifts, and talents.

Ask your pastor if he is willing to go preach at another church for free or at a discount? If he will not do this, why should he expect you to offer your services free or at a discount? As with any consumer, pastors pay for what they want, and if they want your gift or service, they will pay for it.

As I stated before: Get your money!

CHAPTER 13

The Manuscript

It troubles me when I hear Christians say things like: "This is my season." "This is my set time to be blessed." I understand the power of a confession of faith but I also know, that making statements like this can weaken your faith, especially if it is not God's appointed time to bless you.

REASON 23

Wealth stays in the pulpit and seldom reaches the pews because... we don't understand God's timing.

There is a reason why God allowed words like due season, set time, an appointed time to be written in the scriptures. If you look closely at the meaning of these words, you will notice that they all have to do with a scheduled time. Just like a baby is due nine months after conception, God's time to bless you is also an appointed time. A mother can say in the fourth month of her pregnancy that it is her time to deliver and rush to the hospital. However, she will be sent home for five more months because her baby is not due yet.

When we confess these spiritual sayings we are setting ourselves up for disappointment. God has a time for you to be blessed and it will not come any sooner than He has predestined. A confession can't make it happen any sooner, neither can an offering. It will only happen in God's time. God is the only one who can change the timing or speed it up.

Just as God performs miracles as He wills. He blesses us at His will. Rest assured, that it is His will for us to be blessed and stay in faith. If you haven't received what you have prayed for yet, don't fear, it just might not be your season.

In the natural, a farmer cannot plant a seed on Sunday and expect a harvest on Monday. A farmer knows that there is a time of weeding, watering, and waiting until the time of the harvest. Like a farmer, we must get rid of the weeds (doubt, sin, unforgiveness), we must water (continuing to speak God's word over our lives) and we must W.A.I.T. (work anticipating irrefutable transformation).

Galatians 6:9 amplified:

And let us not lose heart and grow weary and faint in acting nobly and doing right, for in due time and at the appointed season we shall reap, if we do not loosen and relax our courage and faint.

When you believe God will fulfill His promises in your life, it's going to take faith and patience. The reason why God says not to lose heart and grow weary is because His blessings don't always show up instantly. God wants us in position to receive His blessings. Sowing financial seeds and making faith confessions doesn't automatically mean you're in position.

We have to learn to hear from God concerning what He wants us to do, obey what He tells us, and wait. Waiting doesn't mean to stop and take a seat. We must do what we know to do, as we wait to hear further instruction from the Lord.

When it comes to prosperity, we must understand that it will seldom come in lump sums. This is not to say that it's impossible for you to receive a lump sum of money. You may receive a settlement or an inheritance, but normally increase starts to show up gradually as you work and build. The bible says that "we go from faith to faith and from glory to glory" so our diligence plays a key role in our success.

REASON 24

Wealth stays in the pulpit and seldom reaches the pews because... we've placed the gift above the giver.

In Ephesians 4:8 the Bible says: "God gave gifts unto men". The gifts he's referring to are Pastors, Teachers, Apostles, Evangelists, and Prophets. Some Christians have placed these gifts (men) above God.

You may have noticed that many preachers in the Body of Christ have reached celebrity status. They are celebrities because we have made them celebrities. The only way you can be deemed a celebrity is to have fans, and this is where we come in. We applaud them, we stand when they enter a room, we take pictures with them and we have even had them autograph our Bibles.

Some people in the church act like groupies so much that the pastors have to walk with an entourage of bodyguards. We want to point fingers at the pastors for having bodyguards, but they need bodyguards because their fans are out of control.

We've idolized our pastors and put God on the back burner. We'd rather be in "the clique" with our pastor than to be in a relationship with God. We have pleaded with God to give us wealth and prosperity, and God is pleading with us for a relationship with Him once again.

When you're in a relationship with God, there is constant communication, intimacy, instruction, protection, and provision. If you search the scriptures, you will find that the saints had relationships with God, and God provided and supplied their every need. There are people in the Bible like Abraham, Joseph, David, and Solomon who were rich beyond measure and their prosperity stemmed from a deep, intimate relationship with God.

I was angry with my pastors because I felt like they were taking advantage of me, not realizing it was my own fault for putting them and keeping them in a place where they should not have been.

I remember going to see the movie *For Colored Girls* and in one of the scenes, a father murdered his own children. The mother was grief-stricken and her neighbor came to her and told her to take responsibility for what had happened. She knew that her mate was deranged and dangerous, but she decided to live with him and support him and he stole the precious lives of her children.

Some of us have allowed our pastors to take things that are precious to us, like our money, our minds, and our relationships with God. We need to take responsibility for this.

I want you to be honest with yourself and think about the dreams, desires, and people you have placed before God and make the adjustments. Some of us have continued to show support when we know that things are not quite right. Some of us have placed loyalty above deity, and God is jealous.

It is right to love, honor and respect the gifts, but not above the giver. Promise yourself, before you sow another seed, you will consider the soil, and whether it's cultivating you having a stronger relationship with God or cultivating you possessing material things. Please know and understand that a personal intimate relationship with God is the key to total life prosperity.

The last thing I want to say about prosperity is that everyone's definition is different, and people have different reasons why they want to be prosperous. Your definition of prosperity may be a billion dollars in the bank, a Bentley and a house in the Bahamas. For someone else the definition may mean the ability to pay for their children's college education, or maybe to travel the world, or to be able to adopt and care for abandoned children.

The point of it all is, God will give us the desires of our hearts when we delight in Him, trust in Him, and Give Him the glory for what He's doing in our lives. All God wants is the glory. All God wants is praise. All God wants is for us to lift up His name, so that all men can be drawn unto Him. God will give each of us our own definition of prosperity, whether it is a mansion or a minivan doesn't matter, as long we partner with God in winning the lost.

It is my prayer that you take the wisdom and instructions in this book and apply them to your life. I have said many things that may help you lay hold to God's promise of prosperity.

Most importantly, I want you to know God care's about your financial well-being. He does not want you to be taken advantage of by people in the world or in the church. He can increase your finances, but you must listen to Him and keep your heart right before Him.

I hope you have identified the areas in your mind that need to change, where the prosperity message is concerned. I hope you will begin the renewal process.

In closing, I want you to promise me that no matter what happens in your life, you will never give up on God or His promises. Things may not happen the way you think they should happen or in a way that makes sense to you, but if you hold up your end, by doing the things that God says in His Word, in conjunction with the things I have shared in this book, you can expect a positive outcome.

I always think of my mother when it comes to prosperity. To me, she was *prosperity in motion*. She struggled most of her life and was making about $600 a month. Yet, she remained faithful to God and His Word and God blessed her beyond her wildest dreams. She was able to buy a brand new house with cash. She furnished it without taking out a loan. All her bills were paid in full and she had no debt.

The one thing that was significant about my mother is that she didn't mention her blessings without first giving God the glory.

She was always willing to help anyone in need. This is true prosperity. She lived her life the way God intended, with abundant bountiful blessings, before she passed away. Perhaps it took a while for the prosperity to come, but it did and she even left an inheritance for all of her children.

Just like a family keeps secrets from outsiders, we in the Body of Christ have kept our secrets and issues hidden under the carpet. How can we ever experience true healing and restoration if we never address our issues?

This book has addressed the issues within the prosperity message. I pray that the preachers and teachers of prosperity as well as the people in the pews will do a self-examination and find that prosperity is a promise made to all of God's children.

God wants prosperity to flow throughout the Body of Christ and to continue outside the doors of the church. In these tough economic times, people need to know that God is not only a healer and a deliverer, but He is also a provider.

About the Author

Leah Pride is an ever budding talent and a jewel to the Body of Christ. She has served as a ghostwriter for many accomplished producers, aspiring authors, directors, and artists in the entertainment industry. Leah is also a published author with a series of books, dismantling the most taboo topics in pop culture and in the church. She is known for her tenacity in tackling controversial subjects and touching on sensitive issues without bias, prejudice, or offense.

Pride is a firm believer that theatre and cinema are effective ways to convey the message of Christ. As a veteran of her craft, Leah skillfully combines the elements of excitement, drama, inspiration, sex, scandal, and suspense to create thought-provoking scenarios with a purpose. Her mission is to inform, educate, inspire and empower others through the arts.

To correspond with Leah Pride,
you may write to her at:

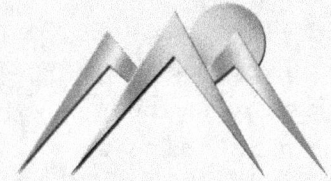

This Rock Entertainment

Email her at
thisrockentertainment@gmail.com

Or visit her websites at:
www.LeahPride.com
&
www.This-Rock.com

www.ingramcontent.com/pod-product-compliance
Lightning Source LLC
Chambersburg PA
CBHW052057070526
44584CB00017B/2229